Gerontology
in Theological Education

Gerontology
in Theological Education

Barbara Payne, PhD
Earl D. C. Brewer, PhD
Editors

The Haworth Press
New York • London

Gerontology in Theological Education has also been published as *Journal of Religion & Aging*, Volume 6, Numbers 1/2 1989.

The Haworth Press, Inc., 10 Alice Street, Binghamton, NY 13904-1580
EUROSPAN/Haworth, 3 Henrietta Street, London WC2E 8LU England

Library of Congress Cataloging-in-Publication Data

Gerontology in theological education.

   "Gerontology in theological education has also been published as Journal of religion & aging, volume 6, numbers 1/2, 1989." – T.p. verso.
   Includes bibliographical references.
   1. Church work with the aged – Case studies. 2. Gerontology – Study and teaching – United States – Case studies. 3. Theology – Study and teaching – United States – Case studies. 4. Aging – Religious aspects – Christianity – Case studies. I. Payne, Barbara P. II. Brewer, Earl D. C.
BV4435.G47   1989   261.8'3426'071173   89-11077
ISBN 0-86656-948-0

Gerontology
in Theological Education

CONTENTS

Acknowledgements   xi

Foreword   xiii
        Neal S. Bellos

PART 1: INTRODUCTION   1

Introduction and Suggestions for Use   3
        Barbara Payne, PhD

Gerontology in Theological Educational (GITE) Model   6
Project Organization   7
Impacting Faculty   8
Implications and Suggestions for Use   9

A National Study of Gerontology in Theological Education   15
        Earl D. C. Brewer, PhD

Involvement of Gerontology   15
Courses on Aging   16
Aging in Contextual Education   19
Continuing Education and Older Adults   20
Relations with Other Agencies   20
Plans for the Future   21
Additional Comments   23
Syllabi of Courses on Aging   25

PART 2: INNOVATIVE PROGRAMS   31

Interdenominational Theological Center: Curriculum Responses to Gerontology   33
        Thomas J. Pugh, PhD

Interdenominational Theological Center: Impacting the Black Church for Ministries with the Elderly   39
Mance C. Jackson, DMin

Understanding the Black Church   40
Recruiting and Training in the Black Church   43
Conclusions   47

Luther Northwestern Theological Seminary: Program in Aging   49
Melvin A. Kimble, PhD

History of the Development of the Program in Aging   50
Course Content   52
Degree Programs   53
Special Programs   55
Aging Program Leadership   56
Future Plans   56

Nashotah House: Gerontology and the Curriculum at a Small Episcopal Seminary   59
Charles F. Caldwell, PhD

Pittsburgh Theological Seminary: A Project in Gerontology   67
Edward A. Powers, PhD
Thomas B. Robb, PhD
Susan N. Dunfee, PhD

History of Aging-Related Offerings   68
Courses and Special Programs   70
Denominational Policy and Programming   71
Student Training in Aging   72
Future Plans and Discussion   72

Presbyterian School of Christian Education: Center on Aging   75
Henry C. Simmons, PhD

A Sense of Vision   76
First Initiatives   77
Emphasis on "Aging" in the Curriculum   78

Research   81
Relationship with the Denomination   81
Distinctiveness of an Educational Focus   82
Conclusion   86

Saint Paul School of Theology: Aging Studies   **89**
     David B. Oliver, PhD

The Seminary   89
The History   90
Relation to Other Seminaries and Gerontology Centers   90
Developing Content and Alternative Educational Strategies   91
Saint Paul Graduates in Religious Gerontology   100
Research Connecting Religion and Aging   100
Community Involvement   101

**Southwestern Baptist Theological Seminary and Baylor
University: Ministerial Gerontological Education**   **103**
     Ben E. Dickerson, PhD
     Dennis R. Myers, PhD
     Lucian E. Coleman, Jr., EdD
     Derrel R. Watkins, EdD

Gerontology at Baylor University   104
Gerontology at Southwestern Baptist Theological
     Seminary   109
The Baylor and the Southwestern Seminary Reciprocal
     Relationship   113
Contributory Factors in Maintaining a Viable Relationship
     Between the University and Seminary   118
Issues in the University-Seminary Relationship   119
Conclusions   121

PART 3: AN ANNOTATED BIBLIOGRAPHY   **123**

Gerontology and Religion: An Annotated Bibliography   **125**
     Barbara Payne, PhD

Gerontology and Applied Practices   126
Theological Disciplines and Clergy Practices   151

ABOUT THE EDITORS

Barbara Payne, PhD, is Professor of Sociology and Director of the Gerontology Center at Georgia State University in Atlanta. Past President of the Association for Gerontology in Higher Education, Dr. Payne is also the first president and founder of the Southern Gerontological Society. Her publications related to religion and aging include three books: *The Meaning and Measurement of Commitment to the Church*, *Love in the Later Years*, and *The Protestant Parish*.

Earl D. C. Brewer, PhD, MDiv, is Charles Howard Candler Professor Emeritus of Sociology and Religion, Candler School of Theology, Emory University, Atlanta, Georgia. In the mid-1970s, he developed and taught a course on religion and aging in the Candler School of Theology that was part of the Gerontology in Seminary Training (GIST) project of the National Interfaith Coalition on Aging (NICA). He also serves as an adjunct faculty member of the Gerontology Center at Georgia State University.

Acknowledgements

This project would not have been possible without the colleague-ship and cooperation of many persons. To name a few is to miss many who contributed.

This collection reports on the national view of Gerontology in Theological Education. The majority of the seminaries in the United States participated in a survey. Faculty members involved in six programs across the country wrote up accounts of innovative work going on. Their reports are included here.

We are indebted to the entire Georgia State University Gerontology Center staff: to Brooks McLamb for his skilled fiscal management and editing of the publications; to Virginia Erhardt for research assistance and editing; to Barbara Patterson for the long hours and careful attention to the preparation of the three manuscripts; to Najah Head for assistance in the preparation of the manuscripts and supervision of the myriad additional tasks and activities in the center caused by the project; to Adria Alston-Wheeler for her good humored willingness to help each of us with our "project" needs.

Other members of Georgia State University have provided services and support. Special mention should go to Clyde W. Faulkner, Dean of the College of Arts and Sciences; and Mr. Clyde Appling, Director of Grants and Contracts.

Last but not least has been the guidance and support from the Administration on Aging throughout the project. Mrs. Sue Wheaton has been especially helpful.

Barbara Payne, PhD
Earl D. C. Brewer, PhD

Foreword

Gerontology in Theological Education (GITE) was a project developed in the Gerontology Center of Georgia State University under a grant from the Administration on Aging. It involved students and faculty from the three seminaries in Atlanta: Candler School of Theology, Columbia Seminary and the Interdenominational Theological Center.

The information from the project is available in two publications. One publication reports on a nationwide study of theological schools, six case studies of innovative programs in gerontology within seminaries and an extensive annotated bibliography.

The second publication reports on the Atlanta experience in curriculum development, post-doctoral work, participation by faculty in gerontology and in theological disciplines and involvement of students from the three seminaries.

During the two-year project, there was a continuing relationship with the Association for Gerontology in Higher Education (AGHE). This included dissemination of results through regular program sessions and pre-conference meetings, the organization of an approved Study Section on Religion and Aging and an increase in the number of theological schools becoming members of AGHE.

Issues of the newsletter, *Message*, reported on the progress of the project, and this publication has become the approved newsletter of the Study Section on Religion and Aging.

Both publications should be useful to administrators and faculty in developing and evaluating programs of gerontology in theological education. They could appropriately find places for these publications in libraries and on reading lists of courses dealing with gerontology in seminaries and in gerontology centers.

The Association for Gerontology in Higher Education welcomes

xiii

these publications and the movement of theological schools to concern themselves with the emerging needs of the increasing numbers of older adults in society and religious congregations.

Neal S. Bellos
President, 1987-88
Association for Gerontology in Higher Education

PART 1: INTRODUCTION

Part 1 contains two introductory pieces. One is a general introduction to the whole project together with suggestions for use and implications for developing gerontology in theological curricula. It includes references to both parts of this material. The second shows the results of a brief survey of seminaries in the United States. These articles provide an overview of the Gerontology in Theological Education (GITE) Project. They should be helpful in moving through the two parts and in making use of them in future work on aging concerns in seminaries. The summaries have been provided by the Editors.

Introduction and Suggestions
for Use

Barbara Payne, PhD

SUMMARY. The need for the training of clergy in gerontology is explored. The history of efforts in this field is developed. Against this background the Gerontology in Theological Education (GITE) project is described. Some implications and suggestions for use in seminaries covers the two parts of the report.

The purpose of this introduction is to set the stage and background of the project. It will refer to materials which appear in the two parts of this report. There are also suggestions about the implications and use of the project results.

The graying of America and of our churches is a demographic revolution comparable to that created by the "baby boom" between 1945 and 1955. The proportion of persons 65 years of age and older has grown from 4% of the population in 1900 to 12% in 1988 and is expected to grow to 17% by the year 2000. Until the middle of the 21st century the increase in life expectancy after age 65 and the aging of the "baby boomers" are expected to result in an unprecedented growth rate among the elderly population.

Sooner or later the age changes in society will affect every individual and institution. We are already experiencing the impacts on health care, intergenerational relationships, the family, the labor force, public policy, the political system, and religious organizations.

Only recently have the age changes in the membership of the major religious organizations in the United States become visible. National Protestant, Catholic and Jewish agencies report that most

---

Barbara Payne is Director of the Gerontology Center, Georgia State University.

3

local congregations have 25% to 35% of their members over 65 years of age, two to three times as many as in the general population. These older members tell us that their faith is very important to them.[1] They support their church and have confidence in their religious leaders.[2] Clergy of all faiths can expect to serve congregations with an aging membership. It seems strange then, that the clergy receive little gerontology in their professional education. For the religious community, it becomes a missional imperative to prepare seminary students to serve churches with an increasing number of older members and to provide leadership in an aging society.

In the more than two decades since Title IV of the Older Americans' Act (1965) initiated career preparation programs in gerontology, training for a wide range of professionals has been established in over two hundred institutions of higher education. None of these were seminaries. Although courses for multidisciplinary gerontology certificates and degree programs have been developed in colleges and universities, most seminaries do not include behavioral science content on aging within their courses. This omission may be attributed, in part, to the source of funding (goverrment), the separation of church and state issue, the scant attention of gerontologists to the role of religion in the aging process and limited recognition of churches/synagogues as support systems for older persons.

There have been scattered efforts to respond to the religious gap in gerontological training. The first major, systematic effort was made by the National Interfaith Coalition on Aging (NICA), a national organization of representatives of Protestant, Catholic and Jewish boards and agencies. In 1974, NICA conducted a national survey of aging programs under religious auspices, including seminaries and schools of theology.[3] They found an overall inadequacy of gerontological course content with none in the curricula of many schools. Although 110 of the responding institutions offered at least one course with an emphasis on gerontology, most of these were applied courses, such as congregational ministry or pastoral care. Few of them reported courses with psychosocial content. To encourage seminaries to include more aging content in seminary training NICA conducted the (1974-1976) project GIST (Gerontology in Seminary Training) supported by a grant from the Administration on Aging. Faculty members from forty seminaries who participated in the GIST program developed projects dealing with gerontology and ministry. These were presented at The 1979 National Conference on Aging, Spiritual Well-Being and Education. Abstracts and articles about these projects were published in a special issue of *Theological Education* (1980).[4]

A decade later we updated the NICA study with a national survey of the 153 accredited seminaries in the United States. As a part of a larger grant, Gerontology in Theological Education, supported by the Administration on Aging, we found some increase in courses and types of curriculum involvement in gerontology and heightened interest in the relevancy of aging issues in theological education. Materials collected from the study may be seen in this publication. As a part of the larger study, eight faculty members prepared and presented in-depth reviews of gerontology on their campuses at the first meeting of AGHE's section on religion and aging in March, 1988. These innovative programs are included as part of this publication.

In 1982, Robert Carlson conducted a study of 13 Episcopal seminaries and found that the seminaries included some aging issues in one or more pastoral care courses and aging experience as an option in field education.[5] Although faculty members showed interest in discussing the place of aging in their courses, they also expressed concern about adding to the pressures on their class time and the limited elective options for students.

The American Association of Retired Persons' (AARP) Interreligious Liaison Office launched a writing project to help religious bodies, including theological seminaries, expand and improve their programs on behalf of older Americans. Scholars in eight theological disciplines were selected to write papers on aging from the perspectives of their own expertise. These papers, published in 1988, make a major contribution to theological resources for curriculum content.[6]

Some of the recent activity related to seminary training includes: (1) the establishment of gerontology programs and centers at St. Paul Seminary, Yale Divinity School, Southwestern Baptist, Pittsburgh Presbyterian Seminary, Luther Northwestern Seminary and The Presbyterian School of Christian Education; (2) the establishment of joint certificate programs in gerontology between a university gerontology center and a local seminary such as Georgia State University with the Candler School of Theology at Emory University, Baylor with Southwestern Baptist Seminary, and Luther Northwestern with North Texas State.

There is also a growing recognition by the Aging Network of the role that clergy and congregations can play in providing support services for older persons, especially the frail elderly. The research of Shelly Tobin et al. demonstrated the feasibility and potential for local congregations working with aging agency staff and programs.[7]

The need for including aging in the professional education of the clergy seems clear. The seminaries of all faiths are facing a demographic and missional mandate. Clergy need knowledge about the aging process, social service needs and resources, intergenerational issues, and, also, communication and counseling skills with the elderly to be effective in their profession. It was in response to this gerontological gap in theological education and the omission of religion in gerontological curriculum that Georgia State University's Gerontology Center planned and implemented the model described in the following sections.

GERONTOLOGY IN THEOLOGICAL EDUCATIONAL (GITE) MODEL

In 1986, the Gerontology Center at Georgia State University developed and implemented a model project for introducing aging content into theological education, funded by a grant from the Administration on Aging. The model calls for a joint effort between seminaries in the Atlanta area and a university gerontology center to introduce aging content into seminary education. The major goals of the model are: (1) to raise the awareness of faculty members and administrators to respond to the age structure changes in congregations and society; (2) to involve seminary faculty as post-doctoral gerontology fellows and to deliver lectures on the impact of aging on theological disciplines; (3) to develop and conduct a basic gerontology course sequence and modules in gerontology for seminary education; and (4) to review and develop library holdings in gerontology and religion and aging.

The case of Atlanta involved three seminaries: The Candler

School of Theology, Emory University which is the largest of the United Methodist Seminaries with an enrollment of over 700 representing several denominations and an ecumenical faculty of 53; Columbia Theological Seminary, one of 10 Presbyterian schools of theology, which has an enrollment of over 500 students and a faculty of 33; and, The Interdenominational Theological Center which is an ecumenical cluster of seminaries representing predominately black denominations with an enrollment of 350 students and 21 full-time and 27 part-time faculty members. It is a part of Atlanta University Center.

PROJECT ORGANIZATION

To implement the model project required institutional support from the deans or presidents of the seminaries and a consortium-like arrangement between the participating seminaries and a university gerontology center. In the Georgia State University project, there were already in place several organizational agreements that facilitated this process: (1) a formal agreement between the Atlanta academic institutions for cross-listing courses and exchange of course credits; (2) a joint gerontology certificate program; and (3) ten years of experience in offering courses on aging and congregations through the Gerontology Center and the Atlanta Theological Association.

When the project goals and operational plan were developed, the project directors met separately with the deans of the three seminaries to review the model project and to formalize their support and contribution to the project.

An advisory committee was established to review curriculum for aging content, recommend procedural policy, assist in recruitment of students, publicize the program and monitor the progress of the project. The committee included the project directors, a representative from each seminary, a representative from Catholic family services, a Rabbi, the executive director of the state Council of Churches, the director of the state office of aging and two gerontology professors.

The Gerontology Center director and staff were responsible for the administration of the project.

IMPACTING FACULTY

Although the project was introduced to the seminaries by the University's Gerontology Center, that is, from an outside organization, it was structured to involve faculty members in its implementation. Rather than sending a gerontologist to the seminaries, the seminary deans appointed a faculty member from each seminary as a post-doctoral gerontology fellow in the Georgia State University Gerontology Center for one year. They selected highly respected, tenure-track professors who will continue to impact faculty and curriculum. They were Nancy Ammerman, professor of sociology of religion, Edward Trimmer, professor of Christian education and Thomas Pugh, professor of pastoral care.

The fellows reviewed their seminaries' curricula for aging content and emphasis; participated as post-doctoral fellows in core gerontology courses; supervised seminary student projects and the aging course of study; met with selected faculty within their institutions about introducing course content on aging and the implications of aging for their area of instruction; planned the content of a course of study in aging at their seminaries; participated in a series of gerontology faculty development seminars and consultations; and reported to their deans and at faculty meetings about the progress of the project and its meaning. Their reports may be seen in the second publication.

To raise consciousness further, a short survey was mailed to 109 faculty members requesting information about the relation of their courses to aging; opinions about the need for aging courses and content now and in the future; and a short attitude/knowledge test. The report may be seen in the second publication.

For continuous impact, an information newsletter, "MESSAGE," was established. It introduced the project, reported on progress and included selected bibliographies. It continues to be published as the official newsletter of the Section on Religion and Aging of The Association on Gerontology in Higher Education.

After the project had been in process for six months, the project directors reported on it at regular faculty meetings of the seminaries. This proved to be the best timing to reinforce faculties' knowledge about the project and to reflect the support and interest in integrating gerontology into seminary education.

A major method of impacting the faculties of the three seminaries was to involve them in the model curriculum. Several faculty members delivered lectures on aging from their disciplinary perspectives and served as panel members. These papers appear in the second publication.

Adequate library resources are essential to develop and support academic programs and courses in any new field of study, such as gerontology and its relation to religious practices. Determining what is "adequate" or basic requires a plan of acquisitions.

The GITE project plan was to collect a listing of the library holdings of the Atlanta seminaries and Georgia State University on gerontology, religion and aging and on aging in the theological disciplines. These lists, reviewed and analyzed by gerontologists in theological education, provided the bases for comparison with other institutions. Recommendations and financial support for basic acquisitions were developed as a part of this project. The annotated bibliography (in this publication) grew out of this work.

IMPLICATIONS AND SUGGESTIONS FOR USE

The overall purpose of this project has been to provide information which might be useful to those interested in planning the introduction or improvement of gerontological material in the curricula of theological schools. The specific purpose of this section is to aid administrators and faculty to locate materials in both publications which relate to their gerontological concerns. The first suggestion would be to scan the articles in both publications. The second idea would be to identify the items reviewed here which apply to your seminary situation. In this manner, the implications and contributions of this project may be fruitful as you plan for gerontology in various aspects of the work of your school. The third point would be to share this report with faculty members, especially those involved in or interested in the concerns of the elderly in congregations and communities. Students should be encouraged to look at it, also.

The authors of this report are aware of the pressures on theological schools to respond to this and that emerging problem or issue. This becomes a practical matter of adding courses or modules, allocating time and talent, adding new faculty members, securing funds, seeing this concern in relation to others, and so on. It is hoped that this report will be helpful in moving through some of these issues and will be encouraging in seeing what others have done.

Here are a few suggestions about the implications of this project for your seminary.

1. Faculty now teaching an introductory course in religion and aging will want to review both publications with special attention to the suggestions about an introductory course in the second publication.

2. Faculty members interested in adding modules or sections on aging concerns in existing courses may profit from some of the introductory course material related to their disciplines. Also, the articles on theological disciplines and practices in the second publication will be useful.

3. In both courses and modules, the annotated bibliography in this publication will be a resource.

4. Librarians may want to check their holdings in this area against the annotated bibliography. It is intended to be helpful in, bringing theological school library resources up to a starting level. Inter-seminary, seminary-university and seminary-gerontological center relations may be useful in supplementing library resources.

5. A discussion of these materials by the entire faculty will lay the groundwork for progress in this area. Someone could prepare a summary or digest of the volumes in preparation for such discussions. The volumes could be placed in the library or passed around the faculty for further study.

6. Part of this discussion could be an effort by the faculty to get in touch with their own aging and its implications for their approach to teaching in this area.

7. Special attention should be paid to the results of the research both in the Atlanta seminaries (see second publication) and in all accredited seminaries in the United States (in this publication). These findings could become mirrors reflecting situations in individual seminaries.

8. The report on good things going on in eight situations (in this publication) should be stimulating and encouraging. Each of these cases may provide clues, both positive and negative, to future development in your situation.

9. The articles on various theological disciplines and clergy practices (see second publication) may stimulate further work in these areas. In this connection, faculty members interested in the relation of aging and world religions should consult James B. Boskey et al., *Teaching About Aging.*[8] This helpful material is a result of another project sponsored by the Administration on Aging.

10. The present project indicates development in aging concerns in field education, clinical pastoral education, supervised ministry in homes, congregations, and various community and institutional settings for elderly. This aspect of theological education should be reviewed and expanded.

11. Continuing education opportunities abound in this field. Since most present clergy went through seminary with little or no training in ministries to and with the elderly, the need for continuing education is enormous. Each theological school should review its present program and plan for a fuller future in this area.

12. A highlight of the Atlanta experience was a field trip to a rural community and its elderly (see second publication). Often these neglected and bypassed older persons need special care which rural congregations could provide. Seminaries should take special note of their opportunities here.

13. The Atlanta experience (see second publication) showed the importance of intermingling gerontological disciplines (physical, biological, psychological, sociological, economic, political, etc.) and theological disciplines and clergy practices (theology, scripture, tradition, ethics, religious education, psychology of religion, sociology of religion, pastoral care, preaching, congregational programs, etc). Care should be taken to have these dimensions of understanding and ministry adequately involved in the total emphasis on the concerns of the elderly.

14. Lectures by visiting scholars or clergy often excited and involved both faculty and students in the cases reviewed in this publication. Encouraging student involvement in this relatively new field is important.

15. Research in religion and aging and in the various disciplines and practices in seminary education was represented in a limited way in this project. Yet the survey in the Atlanta seminaries (see second publication) and in accredited seminaries in the United States (in this publication) produced results suggestive of future work. Seminaries, as religious institutions, ordinarily do not get governmental grants for research in any area. This means that special searches in religious organizations and foundations would need to be mounted for research and support funds for expansion in this field. A study of the financial support or lack of it for the cases in this publication would be instructive.

16. Consortia type relationships between seminaries and with universities and gerontology centers have proved fruitful in the development of programs and in the training utilization of faculty resources, especially post-doctoral studies in gerontology.

17. The demographic trends in congregations and communities are for more people over 65 years of age in the future. As seminaries and their faculties and students face the future, the multi-aged composition of both congregations and communities with more older and fewer younger people will confront them with the necessity of rethinking and refeeling conceptions of theological education and ministry practices. A paradigm shift toward older persons is upon us. According to the national survey (in this publication) most seminaries are planning for this future with eagerness. That future is now.

NOTES

1. Louis Harris, *Aging in the Eighties: America in Transition*. (Washington, DC: National Council on the Aging), 1981; Presbyterian Panel, *The October, 1980 Questionnaire: Ministry with Older Adults in the United Presbyterian Church*. (New York: United Presbyterian Church U.S.A.), 1980.

2. The Gallup Poll, *Religion in America*, Report 259. (Princeton, NJ: The Gallup Report), 1987.

3. Thomas C. Cook, *The Religious Sector Explores Its Mission in Aging: A Survey of Programs for the Aging Under Religious Auspices, A Final Report*. (Athens, GA: National Inter-faith Coalition on Aging), 1977.

4. J.H. Ziegler (Ed.), *Theological Education*, Vol. XVI, No. 3, Special Issue. (Vidalia, OH: The Association of Theological Schools), 1980.

5. Robert W. Carlson, The Episcopal Seminaries and Aging: A Survey of

Episcopal Seminaries and Schools of Theology as to Teaching and Training in the Field of Ministry to the Aged. *Journal of Religion & Aging*, Vol. 1, No. 4, Summer, 1985.

6. E.A. Powers (Ed.), *Aging Society: A Challenge to Theological Education*. (Washington, DC: Interreligious Liaison Office, American Association of Retired Persons), 1988.

7. Shelly Tobin, J.W. Ellor & S.M. Anderson-Ray, *Enabling the Elderly: Religious Institutions Within the Community Service System*. (Albany, NY: State University of New York Press), 1986.

8. James B. Boskey, S.C. Hughes, R.H. Manley & D.H. Wimmer, *Teaching About Aging*. (Washington, DC: University Press of America), 1982.

A National Study of Gerontology in Theological Education

Earl D. C. Brewer, PhD

SUMMARY. A brief questionnaire was mailed to the accredited seminaries in the United States. The purpose was to find out what theological schools were doing in gerontological education. The response was excellent and there was evidence of increasing involvement in this area. Yet, seminary leaders felt that more should be done to keep abreast of our aging society and congregations.

As part of the project on Gerontology in Theological Education, a brief questionnaire was mailed to 153 accredited seminaries in the United States. There were 113 responses distributed among several communions (see Table 1).

INVOLVEMENT OF GERONTOLOGY

The seminary leaders were asked about the involvement of the curriculum in gerontology or material dealing with the concerns of the elderly. The nature of the involvement and the percentage of seminaries claiming that involvement can be seen in Table 2.

The greatest involvement of seminaries (82.3%) in programs dealing with the concerns of older persons was in the areas of field education, internships and other forms of contextual education (Item 3). The least involvement (26.5%) was for continuing education (Item 4). This is especially disturbing since most current clergy

---

Earl D. C. Brewer is Charles Howard Candler Professor Emeritus of Sociology and Religion, Candler School of Theology, Emory University.

had little training in gerontology in their seminary days. Only a third of the seminaries claimed working relationships in gerontology with other seminaries, gerontology centers or aging networks (Items 5 and 6). Yet 6 out of 10 schools had courses (Item 1) and nearly 7 out of 10 had modules (Item 2) in gerontology. In addition, nearly half claimed plans for the future in this area (Item 7).

COURSES ON AGING

Sixty-nine of the 113 responding seminaries reported 103 specific courses dealing with various aspects of theological education and the concerns of older persons. Although these exhibit a variety of titles, they have been tabulated under six categories (see Table 3).

Most of these courses were in the "practical" or applied side of the curriculum. This is to be expected. Yet efforts in different forms of ministry need to be rooted in theology and ethics, to say nothing of scripture and tradition. It is to be hoped that concerns for and with the last third of life will permeate the theological disciplines as they do the various clergy practices.

Although we did not ask when these courses were started, there

TABLE 1

```
Roman Catholic................................31
Nondenominational or interdenominational......14
Presbyterian..................................12
Baptist.......................................11
Methodist.....................................11
Episcopal..................................... 7
Lutheran...................................... 7
Christian (Disciples of Christ)............... 4
United Church of Christ....................... 4
Reformed Church in America.................... 2
Churches of Christ............................ 1
Christian Reformed............................ 1
Church of the Brethren........................ 1
Church of God................................. 1
Church of the Nazarene........................ 1
Eastern Orthodox.............................. 1
Mennonite..................................... 1
Moravian...................................... 1
Quaker........................................ 1
Unitarian Universalist........................ 1
```

TABLE 2

Nature of Involvement	Percentage Claiming such Involvement
1. Do you have courses dealing with the concerns and needs of older persons and ministry to and with them?	61.1
2. Does material dealing with older persons appear as part(s) of other courses in the school?	68.1
3. Is work with older persons included in field education, internships and other forms of contextual education?	82.3
4. Does your continuing education program include any workshops or courses on aging persons?	26.5
5. Does your school have working relations on aging with other seminaries or gerontology centers?	31.9
6. Does your school have working relations with the aging networks at the community, country, or state levels?	31.9
7. Do you have plans for the future in the field of aging?	46.0

TABLE 3

Category of Courses	Number of Courses
All Courses	103
1. Ministry and Older Persons	37
2. Gerontology	23
3. Pastoral Care and the Elderly	19
4. Religion, Theology, Ethics and the Elderly	11
5. Christian Education and Older Persons	8
6. Field Education	5

would seem to have been an increase in them during the eighties. Even so, it leaves 54 seminaries reporting no such courses plus an additional 40 not responding to the questionnaire. Also, questions may be raised about the training and background of seminary faculty members in gerontology. Although there are a few outstanding exceptions, most of these courses would appear to be offered by those qualified in various theological disciplines or practices with an interest in applying them to the needs of the elderly.

Admittedly, finding room for a new course in the curricula of seminaries is difficult. Yet this is an important way to respond to the needs of older adults in society and congregations. Considerable development in the number of new courses and in the training of faculties in religious gerontology will doubtless take place in the years ahead.

Modules on Aging in Seminary Courses

Seventy-seven of the 113 responding seminaries indicated that 193 of their courses included some material or modules dealing with older adults (Table 4).

The field of pastoral care and counseling claimed the largest number of courses with some attention to the needs of older persons. Faith and human development and Christian education had some similar emphases and were in second and third places. Death and dying and health care were the only courses with titles relating to gerontology. Theology as a traditional discipline along with ethics was mentioned 12 times. Bible was not mentioned at all and

TABLE 4

Category of Courses	Number of Courses
All Courses	193
1. Pastoral care and counseling	60
2. Faith development and the life course	25
3. Christian education	20
4. Pastoral theology and ministry	14
5. Family ministry	13
6. Death and dying	12
7. Religion, theology, ethics	12
8. Church, society	11
9. Worship and preaching	8
10. Field Education	7
11. Evangelism	3
12. Health care	3
13. Church history	2
14. Church Administration	1
15. Congregational life	1
16. Sexuality	1

church history only twice. The "practical" disciplines were somewhat better represented, especially pastoral care and Christian education. Obviously, less attention is given to the elderly in preaching, evangelism, church administration and field education.

The development of modules in regular seminary courses is an appropriate and feasible response to the growing numbers and needs of older adults in congregations. Much fruitful work in this area would seem to be ahead for the seminaries across the United States.

AGING IN CONTEXTUAL EDUCATION

Ninety-three of the 113 seminaries reported some involvement of the concerns of elderly people in their field or contextual education programs. There were 87 specific settings mentioned for field education dealing with older adults (see Table 5).

Three major impressions result from a study of the responses to the question about the involvement of older adults in field education in seminaries. First, most of the seminaries report programs of field or contextual education. Second, older persons are involved along with other age groups but with no special emphasis. Third, some settings involved older adults directly.

In Table 5, the settings of parishes or congregations and hospitals would seem to involve older persons along with others. The nursing homes and homes for the aged definitely included older people. The

TABLE 5

Settings	Number
All Settings	87
1. Parishes or congregations	19
2. Nursing homes	19
3. Homes for the aged	16
4. CPE settings	10
5. Community agencies	7
6. Hospitals	4
7. Geriatric Centers	3
8. Hospice	3
9. Home visitation	3
10. Long-term health care facility	2
11. A A Group	1

clinical pastoral education settings and community agencies provided special opportunities for contextual education. Only a small number of other settings was reported.

It seems obvious that the older population is receiving as limited attention in contextual education as in classroom endeavors.

CONTINUING EDUCATION
AND OLDER ADULTS

Only thirty seminaries reported some continuing education programs dealing with ministry to and with older adults. This is somewhat surprising since so few practicing clergy had opportunities for training in this field during their seminary days.

The responses pointed to workshops dealing with various themes of concern with older people. These themes were not indicated as fully as for courses and settings for field education. Some of them related to biblical and theological concerns with the elderly. Most dealt with equipping clergy and laity with knowledge and experiences useful in ministries to and with older persons in congregations and communities. It is likely that much more is being done than was reported in this survey.

RELATIONS WITH OTHER AGENCIES

Thirty-six seminaries reported relationships with other agencies in their programs for and with the elderly.

These agencies included gerontology centers in universities, other seminaries, American Association of Retired Persons, retirement facilities, geriatric centers, hospice centers, hospitals, religious organizations, nursing homes, Alzheimer's support networks, governmental agencies, advocacy groups and congregations.

These responses were limited in both number and variety. It seems obvious that most seminaries have only begun to reach out to other agencies in both religious and community settings for support and assistance in programs designed to train clergy and laity to be in ministry to, with and through older adults.

PLANS FOR THE FUTURE

Fifty-two of the 113 responding seminaries reported plans for the future in the area of aging. These plans often involved expanding and strengthening what was already going on. Frequently they included new ventures in curriculum and related opportunities. Some of these plans seemed based more on hope than realistic commitment. Some of the statements of plans for the future might be suggestive.

- A team from AARP will visit our campus to instruct faculty and students on aging issues . . . Lectureship in 1989 — William Clements, speaker . . . Cannot describe. We are at the talking stage, but I hope to have something within eighteen months . . .
- We seek to develop seminars or workshops on life-planning, retirement, and ministry with older persons and consider how we might introduce a course on the concerns and needs of older persons into our present curriculum. Any suggestions, materials, information from your institution will be appreciated as we work toward such integration . . .
- We recognize the great need for training of future ministers in this area especially in the State of Florida. The best we can plan is a single talk every three or four years on the subject to begin to awaken interest in students . . .
- We are developing programs in Intergenerational Ministry in cooperation with the Philadelphia Baptist Association which involve churches in the area and our students . . . Develop more courses for seminary students. Continue to increase size of CPE program in Gerontology. Look at the possibility of adding a retirement center to campus . . .
- I would hope a new faculty member would have an interest in this area and help us develop courses/materials for more effective service to this age group . . .
- A major research facility on aging is to be located in our county, possibly on our campus. We are negotiating the program now. It has been funded for several million dollars a year and is open-ended, for at least 10 years . . .

- We intend to continue the relationship with Georgia State . . .
- I am just beginning to structure a 12 hr. gerontology specialization that will be a concentration in our master's program in
  religious education. The curriculum will include a practicum
  requirement in various sites. A two-week inter-term course
  has also been proposed.
- The introduction of a course on Theology and the Aging – A
  seminar on Religion and the Aging . . .
- Increase our library holdings in the field and work with all the
  faculty to make them aware of the issues and resources related
  to ministry to and with the aging . . .
- We are currently conducting research to be used in writing curriculum materials for older adults to be used in the Church . . .
- Expand specialized course offerings in Master of Divinity curriculum. Recent addition to the faculty has gerontology as part
  of his clinical background and will be recommending ways
  in which this concern may be addressed further in the curriculum . . .
- Our Director of Development is interested in the area and in 2
  years will begin offering a workshop in it . . . Regular classes
  on the topic in Pastoral Care . . . Certificate in Aging through
  the university system. Expansion of curriculum through addition of courses . . .
- Gerontology will continue to be a significant part of the School
  of Psychology and a course will be offered in the School of
  Theology within the Christian Formation and Discipleship
  programs. There are Continuing Education programs that have
  segments dealing with the aging. The four divisions within
  Gerontology Services continue to be strong, two of which
  have just received grants within the last several months. We
  are presently considering the production of video tapes on aging, publishing books in the area (several faculty have books
  or parts of books on the aging), and hosting national conferences on topics of aging . . .
- We are in the process of identifying issues, concerns and data
  about the aged and aging. This will lead to courses, field edu-

cation placements, and some alteration in our seminary internships . . .

- We plan to continue to include the agenda related to the field of aging in our course in Christian education, pastoral care and counseling, worship, preaching, and other forms of ministry, both in the classroom setting as well as in supervised ministry settings. Occasionally we may offer a specific course focused on the needs of older persons . . .
- Develop cooperative graduate degree program(s) in institutional administration. The M.A. in Parish Counseling will include this area. May invite adjunct professors to teach seminars on this subject . . .
- Hope to offer again a Pastoral Care of the Aging course; expect that we shall be attending somewhat more carefully to the needs of the aging as part of our general offerings and requirements . . .
- An endowment in this area would aid expansion. Short of that, our only expansion would be in more electives given by present faculty . . .

ADDITIONAL COMMENTS

Several respondents provided additional remarks regarding their training for ministry to and with the elderly. Here is a selection of those comments.

- It is popular in America to work with people and to study people according to age, sex and interest. And to this end numbers are important. I have an interest in the effective pastoral care of the aging. It is my feeling that a significantly larger study of them will produce data which on analysis we may learn how to be helpful beyond their physical and psychological needs to ultimate meaning and thus include service to the whole persons . . .
- Lobbies need to be organized by churches for the financial concerns of long term care, the need for low income housing, senior citizen subsidized housing, etc . . .

- I am in the process of gathering information from various schools and agencies that will assist me in building curriculum. I appreciate your input and will welcome any and all materials you can forward to me . . .
- I am working with AARP in the religion division on a program (essentially writings on theology and the aging). The book is to appear in the early part of 1988 . . . We should have a consultant — visit of AARP or other group to faculty and administrative council . . .
- The Episcopal Church is not strongly involved with geriatric issues in the New York area. Student interest is not great. Pressure from Bishops and Dioceses would help the marketing of geriatric offerings. More CPE programs should intentionally address gerontology . . .
- I applaud your efforts in this regard and would like to know how the program develops. It is most needed. Perhaps it can be imitated in other areas of the country. We look forward to hearing about it in the years ahead. Please share any information (good or bad) so all can learn . . .
- We are most interested in this issue. With limited resources we are endeavoring to raise consciousness in this area . . .
- Your having sent this questionnaire reminds me that we are not doing nearly enough in the area of aging. I will raise the matter in our Curriculum Committee . . . We do, of course, continue to develop our library and would appreciate any bibliography on aging, religion and aging that would be helpful. We do subscribe to the *Journal of Religion & Aging* . . .

This survey indicates significant recent attention on the part of many seminaries to the presence and needs of increasing numbers of older persons in congregations and society. The good work going on, as reported here, should be helpful to administrators and faculty in renewed efforts to develop and implement curricular programs concerning the problems and possibilities of older persons today and tomorrow.

SYLLABI OF COURSES ON AGING

In the national survey of theological schools, leaders were invited to send syllabi of courses dealing with aging concerns. Many sent complete syllabi and others included catalogue description of courses. The syllabi are too long to include in this brief research report. Yet, a few of the key features may be useful to persons planning new courses in this field as well as those modifying existing courses. There will be a review of the stated purposes and objectives of the courses, methods, resources and faculty background.

Purposes and Objectives

In the syllabi, there were various ways of stating purposes and objectives of the courses. It may be instructive to recount some of these.

- The objectives of the course include the following: (1) students should gain a basic understanding of the biological, psychological, and sociological approaches to the study of aging and their interrelationships; (2) students should become familiar with the history, the concepts, and some of the basic literature of gerontology as a field of study; (3) students should be able to read and critique social-scientific research that will enhance theological reflection and practices of ministry; (4) students should be able to refine further their analytical skills in reading, understanding, conducting and applying research in gerontology to practices of ministries.
- The purpose is to become familiar with gerontological and theological principles and practices as they relate to ministries with, by and to the increasing numbers of older persons in congregations.
- Upon completion of this course, students should be able to: Broaden the student's understanding of the opportunities and challenges of the aging process and the impact of this process on the individual, family, church, and society; increase the student's sensitivity to the spiritual and psychosocial needs of later life and her/his capacity for addressing identified needs

through resource development and/or utilization; develop a defensible theological rationale for ministry with older persons; analyze the implications of the course to the student's own perspective on the realities of aging.

• To introduce the student to the subject of gerontology and to an effective ministry to the older person in American society. Most specifically, to make a beginning in understanding the following: views and theories of aging in a variety of cultures, ancient and modern; the Biblical perspectives on aging and the aged; the physiological and biological changes which take place in the aging process; the psychological changes within the aging process in American society; the socioeconomic changes confronting the older person in American society; the ministry of Word and Sacrament to older persons in our culture; religious, governmental and community sources of aid to the aged; the role of homes for the aged and nursing homes in our culture; problems faced by the aging in American society; retirement, employment, economic security, health and health care, loneliness, institutionalization, etc.; the role of the local church in ministry to the older person; personal characteristics of those who are most effective in ministry to the aged; education among the aged; leisure activities for the older person; and the ministry of the church to the sick and dying among the aged. This would include beginning skills to develop personal qualities requisite to successful work with the older person; to achieve facility in applying Word and Sacrament to the aged; to develop a program of ministry to the aging person from the standpoint of the whole person – spiritual, intellectual, emotional, physical. This program especially related to the local congregation and to develop facility in work among the aged in institutional settings.

• The course is designed to provide an understanding of the various factors that are involved in a ministry with older adults in a congregation. These factors will include some biblical and theological perspectives that will guide the development of programs; an analysis of the implications of the growing numbers of older adults, their contributions and their needs; and will concentrate on ways the congregation can work creatively and meaningfully with older adults. The purpose of the course is to help participants (1) know and understand important biblical and theological perspectives, (2) identify the demographic factors involved in the growing numbers of older adults, (3) relate in a personal way to the aging process in others and in themselves, (4) examine ways congregations are responding to the needs of older adults and (5) understand how to use the many resources that are available to assist in a ministry with older adults.

- Objectives: to identify problems of the senior adult from the biological, sociological and spiritual points of view; to identify the changes that take place in relationships as a person ages; to discuss specific problems faced by persons in the retirement years; to review developmental tasks of persons in the later years; to examine program possibilities in developing a ministry to meet needs of the senior adult; to identify means of meeting the needs of senior adults through the church.

- The purpose of this class is to study the nature and dynamics of pastoral care with older adults. The fastest growing age group in the country (both within and outside of the church), older adulthood represents both a special challenge and a special opportunity for the care of the church. In this class, we will examine foundational issues regarding aging in theology, ethics, and psychology in order better to understand how our care of older adults can represent a fitting enactment of the Christian witness. We will also be concerned, however, with concrete issues of practice: specific means by which the church can care for older adults and by which older adults can especially participate in the care of the church. By the conclusion of the course, students should be able to understand the cultural and theological issues at stake in aging and be able to articulate appropriate programmatic possibilities for the local church in that light.

- It is our overall objective that at the end of the course you will be more aware of your strengths, limits, stereotypes of minis-

try and of older people and that you will have developed some
pastoral skills for working with the elderly and with people of
all ages.
• The course is designed to examine our own attitudes toward
aging and the old; to introduce students to general information
about aging and older persons in society today; to examine the
gifts and needs older adults bring which contribute to the ministry of the church by, with, and for these persons; to consider
models for ministry with older adults with an emphasis on
educational ministry; and to evaluate resources for educational
ministry with older adults.
• The goal of this course is to examine and reflect upon, in a
dialogical context, ideas, insights, and knowledge about older
adult educational ministries and to do so in ways that theory
and practice are brought together.
• This course is intended to be an introduction to the situation of
older adults in American society, particularly within the organized church. Since most of you will find that a sizable proportion of the congregations you serve will be older, much that
we discuss should be useful. There are several minimum
skills, experiences and pieces of information that you should
have to serve older members and their support systems.

Methods

Many teaching methods to achieve the objectives of the courses
were indicated in the syllabi. These included reading, book reviews, papers, journal writing, interviews, observations, small
group discussions, involvement with the elderly, congregational
study, viewing films and videotapes, class participation and examinations. There was sensitivity to joining the methods of empirical
gerontological research and the procedures of theological disciplines and practices. Panel discussions and experts were occasionally used. Overall there was a fresh and lively approach to this
"new kid on the block" in the curricula of seminaries. As might be
expected, there was more emphasis on the traditional lecture
method than any other. Although there was a healthy mixture, the
focus, as might be expected, was more on theological disciplines

and practices than on the biological, psychological and social dimensions of gerontology. This was clearly noted in the session-by-session topics of the courses. While these are too extensive to be reviewed here, they exhibit an awareness of the issues and, in many cases, the need to call in experts on various topics.

Resources

Although there was use made of audio-visual media, the main resource in these courses was the traditional readings, mostly in books. There were excellent reading lists for most of the courses. These are too extensive for review here. Instead attention will focus on required readings. In the annotated bibliography the expected readings in the syllabi are marked with an asterisk. There was a wide variety of authors represented. Only a few (Atchley, Butler, Clements, Bianchi, Hendricks, Boyle, Comfort) were mentioned more than once. There is little standardization of resources in this field.

Faculty Background

These courses on aging concerns are offered in seminaries. Naturally, the faculty will be more expert in theological disciplines and practices than in the various aspects of gerontology. Occasionally, a person with major training in gerontology is a seminary faculty member on a temporary or tenured basis. It is instructive to note the academic backgrounds of faculty members in relation to the themes of courses or modules: Sociology—5; Psychology and Pastoral Care—4; Ministry and Congregational Programs—4; Christian Education—3; Social Work—2; and one each for the following: Biology, Psychology, Political Science; Liturgy, Worship; Psychology and Faith Development; Theology; Church and Community; Church History; Bible; Theology and Spiritual Life; and Preaching.

As gerontological courses, modules and emphases become more common in seminaries, more faculty members will seek training in this field. There is excitement in the prospects for theological and gerontological mixtures in the curricula of seminaries. This review of existing syllabi adds promise for the future.

PART 2: INNOVATIVE PROGRAMS

There was a dissemination conference on Gerontology in Theological Education prior to the 1988 meeting of the Association for Gerontology Higher Education. Several of the innovative programs included here were presented. Others were prepared at the invitation of the Editors.

These are stories of good things going on in theological schools in the field of aging. There are doubtless other innovative programs as well. However, these are enough to provide guidance for the development of gerontology in seminary curricula in various types of settings.

These case studies range from beginning work in the cluster of predominately black seminaries in the Interdenominational Theological Center to the well established and endowed program at the United Methodist Saint Paul School of Theology. The patterns of involvement in the other cases differ considerably. Nashotah House (Episcopal) is an example of the introduction of gerontology into a small seminary. Luther Northwestern (Lutheran) tells the story of the development of a large and well established program.

An outside gerontologist was brought in to introduce gerontology in the Pittsburgh Theological Seminary (Presbyterian). The question there is how much will remain after the outsider is gone. The Center on Aging in the Presbyterian School of Christian Education is one of the oldest programs relating religion and aging. The Southwestern Baptist Theological Seminary and Baylor University show the possibilities and problems in a seminary-university cooperative program in gerontology and theological education.

These are exciting innovative programs in the relatively new field of relating gerontological and theological disciplines and practices.

Interdenominational Theological Center: Curriculum Responses to Gerontology

Thomas J. Pugh, PhD

SUMMARY. The author participated in the year-long program on Gerontology in Theological Education held at Georgia State Gerontology Center. There is a description of I.T.C. and its mission statement. The introduction of a course in Gerontology is described. Although in the area of pastoral care, it is to be team taught and to contain experimental elements.

The Interdenominational Theological Center was an experimental response to a crisis in Black theological education in many related schools, only one of which was accredited—Gammon Theological Seminary. The others operated under the auspices of their denominational colleges.

The context in which I.T.C. was begun, and indeed the first decade of her life, was in a world-wide movement of intentional action led by Black clergy to improve the quality of human relations. The right to nondiscrimination in public travel and to receive other creature comforts was a welcome freedom for Black people. At the same time, if not parallel thereto, significant changes were made in the process of educational administration and housing.

In the midst of these dynamics, Interdenominational Theological Center was born in 1958. It is a cooperative, ecumenical, international, interracial theological experiment. The students of six supporting denominations are taught in one educational curriculum by a common faculty. However, it permits students to be trained in the

Thomas J. Pugh is Professor of Religion and Pastoral Care, Interdenominational Theological Center, Atlanta, GA. He has served, also, as Vice President and Academic Dean at I.T.C.

history and polity of their denominations. Such courses are taught by respective denominational persons approved by the faculty. The I.T.C. is accredited by the Association of Theological Schools and the Southern Association of Colleges and Schools. It is one of the member schools in the United Negro College Fund (UNCF).

Administratively, each of the participating schools (denominations) in the Center is bound by a pattern of cooperation.

> It is cooperation [among] independent, autonomous institutions. Each participating school remains under its own board of trustees. Each retains its own funds and assets.[1]

Each of the original four schools (Gammon, Morehouse, Turner, and Phillip) has a denominational house which accommodates the administrative needs of the Administrative Dean, a liaison person between the denomination and I.T.C. and student housing. The seminaries pay "the Center a fixed fee for the instruction of each student."[2]

> The I.T.C. board of trustees is in complete control of the Center. They elect the President, employ the faculty, determine policies, set the curriculum, and promote the financial welfare of the Center. They hold and manage the Center's property.[3]

The financial resources of the Center are new monies raised especially for the needs of the Center.

I.T.C. is a cooperative theological endeavor to train leaders for service to the churches in the midst of ferment in society. A new model was needed. Black Christian witnesses were not loyal to the structures of theological schools at the time since the religious experiences which dominated theological education excluded them. Critics of the enterprise saw the lack of relevance, as practiced, to the needs of a significant minority group. The question, then, was who will lead them? It was believed that the need for liberation was supported in the Gospel. The issue is how do you make the Gospel relevant for people with "their backs against the wall" who are in quest of liberation. If the first important step taken was cooperation, then the second was the action of the Trustees, April 24, 1973. It was a new purpose statement which said:

. . . The Center, at this juncture in her historical existence, proclaims its intent to pursue the entire course of theological education from the perspective of the Christian faith, as this faith has been expressed in the Black witnessing community . . . consciously affirming the Gospel of Jesus Christ, the Center now seeks to explore the theological motifs of liberation and reconciliation in their ultimate depth and to prepare Christian ministers and teachers to speak and act in that light.[4]

Fifteen years later the purpose of I.T.C. was stated in essentially the same language.

In recent years, I.T.C., like a number of other theological schools, has served a sizable number of second career persons and an increasing number of women. The latter is a recent important change in the world and in the seminary.

This paper is concerned about the seminary's curriculum response to gerontology. There is no doubt about the need. The basic reasons for the concern are that the largest percent of I.T.C.'s graduates become ministers in congregations, communities or military service. And in congregations where most of them serve, the percent of persons over 65 years of age is larger than the general population. Seminaries must train the prospective minister for adequacy in ministry to persons in the congregation who are advancing in age. Gerontology is the label for the phenomenon of old age. "It means the scientific study . . . of aging, involving the processes of aging and senescence, and including the related problems and achievements of older people."[5]

The first three persons who chaired the I.T.C. Board of Trustees, Dr. Henry P. Van Dusen former President of Union Theological Seminary in New York; Dr. Ernest Cadman Colwell, former President of the University of Chicago, and also Vice-President and Dean of Faculties at Emory University, Atlanta; and Bishop B. Julian Smith of the Christian Methodist Episcopal Church, remained in the position until death. The present chairman is a retiree. The board is basically a group of people who are significantly advanced in years.

The current catalog lists eight living faculty persons who are retired. The range of years in this category is five to fifteen years. All of them retired when the mandatory retirement age was sixty-five. They are now ages seventy to eighty. All of these persons have remained active doing other things. One is minister of a church. One has continued teaching via contract. The others are variously engaged in denominational assignments.

A new curriculum at I.T.C. has been in operation for three years. In the planning process for that projected pilgrimage in theological education, a course in gerontology was added. It is in the Department of Pastoral Care. Its title is "Ministry, Theology and Gerontology." Gerontology as defined above has been an evident factor in I.T.C. from its beginning with older people on the Board of Trustees, on the faculty and recently among the students. Despite some awareness of this, including the representation of older people in churches, there is also denial. Now that the number of older persons is significant, more attention will be given to gerontology. Now that the matter cannot be ignored, some denominations are being more and more intentional about it.

The I.T.C. faculty became participants in gerontology in significant ways in the Gerontology Center of Georgia State University. The course "Gerontology in Theological Education" was co-directed by Barbara Payne and Earl D. C. Brewer during 1986-87. As the weekly seminar sessions were held, persons from the I.T.C. faculty participated. They teach in the following disciplines: Liturgy and Worship, Christian Education, Systematic Theology, Pastoral Care and Counseling, Church History, Church and Community, New Testament and Field Education. Five I.T.C. students were enrolled in the seminar. The students received a certificate in gerontology. A course in gerontology was taught in I.T.C. during summer school in 1987. And a course will be taught by the writer in the fall of 1988. This one curriculum course will be taught by the interdisciplinary approach including all of the disciplines and faculty persons involved in the Georgia State program.

Leadership in gerontology at I.T.C. is provided across the curriculum by faculty assignment to meet the need for synthesis of gerontological material into one course directed by the Department of Pastoral Care. In addition, attention is called to special articles and other resources and updating of information in professional journals and encouragement to attend denominational workshops.

Interdenominational Theological Center is a unique theological school located in a privileged and attractive city. It is a cooperative enterprise. It is a member of the Atlanta University Center, Inc., forming a larger cooperative group than the cluster of schools that makes up I.T.C. Atlanta University Center, Inc. is a consortium of seven schools—four undergraduate colleges: two are co-educational (Clark and Morris Brown), one is for males (Morehouse) and one is for females (Spelman); a graduate school of Arts and Sciences and Social Work (Atlanta University); a medical school (Morehouse School of Medicine) and a graduate school of theology (Interdenominational Theological Center). The I.T.C. has theological resources beyond the Atlanta University Center, Inc. These are on the northeast side of the city. Atlanta has three accredited theological schools. They form the Atlanta Theological Association (ATA). There is through this organization professional affiliation with Candler School of Theology in Emory University, Columbia Theological Seminary in Decatur, Georgia, to which is joined Erskine Theological Seminary in Due West, South Carolina.[6]

Clinical Pastoral Education is the experiential theological component of theological education in this vicinity. It is provided by the Georgia Association for Pastoral Care, Inc. The seminaries participate in the governance of the association. They are joined in this responsibility by the Christian Council of Metropolitan Atlanta, Inc., and Emory University School of Medicine. Varieties of needs are met through this aspect of theological education.

The I.T.C. course in gerontology seeks to look at the phenomenon of growing old comprehensively and wholistically. This will include findings in biology, psychology, sociology and theology. The most important thing this course must do is to indicate that the theological significance of gerontology in pastoral work is to demonstrate progressively love toward God, neighbor and self. The theology of gerontology must develop a pastoral perspective. The course will be open to seminarians and Doctor of Ministry students. Gerontology, from this point in time, will be a discipline in which many practicing clergy persons will update themselves in continuing education. The generation gap between the younger clergy person and older lay person has been crowded with blunders. The older people want to share and the minister too often is not comfortable with this. One seminary president wanted to remove some trustees from positions on the board because of old age. He discounted years of valuable service in favor of younger persons. He exercised this prejudice despite the fact that he is himself qualified for membership in the American Association of Retired Persons. This attitude often leads to hurt and destruction of lay persons. Such denial of the growing old phenomenon in the culture will become more difficult with the increase in the older adult population.

It would be a mistake to offer a course in gerontology limited to classroom and library. Clinical or field experience with older persons will enrich the offerings. The experiential aspect of the course being related to field education and audio-visual selections will add to the appeal of this aspect of the course.

Study in gerontology is important to our African students because their older people serve them as wise folks and keepers of the house when the spouses responsible for the house are away or at work. An important way to change curriculum is for students to make faculty aware of their needs. This includes recruiting their peers to participate. We need more information about what ministers are finding in the churches. What is common and what is unique about people in this stage of life? Learning is thought to have value in itself. Might there not be intrinsic value in growing old? Certainly education and learning may need fuller exploration to determine the contributing potential yet to be discovered here. Martin Luther King Jr. said in his "Mountaintop" sermon, "Longevity has its place." Are we clear regarding the place of longevity? If not, we have work to do. And we must be about it.

NOTES

1. Harry V. Richardson. *The Center*, Vol. 1, No. 1 (Spring 1960), p. 4.

2. Op. cit. p. 5.

3. Op. cit. p. 5.

4. Oswald Bronson. "An Historical Overview of the I.T.C." *The Journal of the I.T.C.*, Vol. 1, No. 1 (Fall 1973), p. 6.

5. Walter R. Cunningham & John W. Brookbank. *Gerontology: The Psychology, Biology, and Sociology of Aging.* (New York: Harper & Row), 1988, p. 1.

6. Interdenominational Theological Center 1988-1991 catalog, p. 18.

Interdenominational Theological Center: Impacting the Black Church for Ministries with the Elderly

Mance C. Jackson, DMin

SUMMARY. This is a description of the ways to make contact with Black pastors and lay people in the interest of training in the concerns of older persons. The pastor is the key point of entry into the Black congregation. Unless he/she is contacted first, little success in recruitment is likely. This is in spite of the great unmet needs of Black elderly in congregations and communities.

Through the initiative and under the direction of The Gerontology Center at Georgia State University, several members of the faculty at the Interdenominational Theological Center became involved in a program, Gerontology in Theological Education (GITE). In his case study of seminary curriculum responses to gerontology at the Interdenominational Theological Center, Dr. Thomas J. Pugh provides a description of our theological school which is located approximately two miles from Georgia State University. He discusses some of our institution's responses to GITE's initiatives and challenges. He captures one aspect of The Gerontology Center's outreach into a Black institution in Atlanta. He projects a significant impact on the future of ministry among Black people in the world as he discusses the education of clergy persons

Mance C. Jackson is Associate Professor of Church Administration and Leadership Education and Director of Continuing Education at the Interdenominational Theological Center, 671 Beckwith Street, S.W., Atlanta, GA.

39

for the Black Church in America, in Africa and in other regions of the world served by our graduates.

This paper will describe another aspect of The Gerontology Center's outreach into the Black community. This module on the Black Church was presented to share insights on a cultural phenomenon which is similar to, yet quite different from that known to the average church person in the White community. It is hoped that these insights will enable the leaders to be more effective in the Black Churches.

UNDERSTANDING THE BLACK CHURCH

It is understood in the Black community and fairly well documented that the Black Church in America has its roots in West Africa, that region of the Continent from which slave traders brought Black people to America. These African roots run deep and they are a powerful influence on what is experienced in Black religion in America. The religion of the slave masters was transmitted to the slaves, but the slaves adapted Christianity to meet their needs, to relate to their condition, to reflect their cultural reality. Therefore, even though most Black Churches have a denominational history and identity in common with their White counterparts, the churches are quite different. Two or three examples should suffice to make the point.

The membership in most Black congregations cuts across socioeconomic, class and status lines. Janitors, maids, truck drivers and hospital attendants are often leaders of boards and auxiliaries on which there are public school principals and teachers, doctors, attorneys and corporate executives. These congregations are communities of faith where the members are valued for their faith, and for their commitment to the faith community and not simply for their accomplishments outside of this community.

Most Black congregations are made up primarily of women and children. Ignoring exceptions, adult male membership in Black Churches is usually less than twenty percent of the adult membership. The majority of the boys who grow up in such congregations tend to drop out when they reach their early teen years. If it is acceptable in their biological families, they may attend a church where there is a strong male presence, or they may choose to attend church only on special occasions. Yet, men are expected to carry major leadership responsibilities in Black Churches. In those congregations where they are few in number, and where their leadership skills may be underdeveloped, women naturally bridge the gap.

The pastor is the head of a local congregation. The Black Church is an all-inclusive term for churches owned and controlled by Black Americans. All types of denominational policy are represented. Nevertheless, in a Black Church, the pastor is expected to have the gifts, talents, abilities and skills to lead, guide and direct the congregation in all areas of its life. In metaphorical terms, the "people of God" expect "the called man or woman of God" to guide them in the way God would have them to go. The "sheep" of God's pasture expect the pastor to be the "shepherd," to lead them in the path of righteousness. God's "called" servant, the pastor, is deferred to as the people were expected to be obedient and to defer to Moses and to Aaron in the Scriptures.

These three examples not only point up some of the unique features of the Black Church, they also suggest ways an outsider will approach a Black congregation. The pastor is always the safest point of entry. He/she is not the only point of entry and in many situations, may not be the easiest and most effective point of entry. Yet in terms of community protocol, the pastor is the point of entry. The "shepherd" wants to know what and who is at work in the flock. An outsider who would enter the flock except through the "shepherd" is suspect. A worker in aging who wants a congregation's cooperation will put forth diligent effort to reach the pastor before having serious discussions with any member of the congregation.

Most Black congregations are small, averaging around three hundred members. However, the vast majority of the congregations have fewer than two hundred members. In the major cities in Georgia, large membership churches will have a full-time pastor who spends some time in the office daily and a clerical person who can take telephone messages when he/she is not available during regular working hours. It will be a waste of time, energy, gasoline and psychic motivation to try to "catch" a Black pastor in the office.

The nature of the job makes it impossible for him/her to spend hours in the office on a routine basis. Community needs pull an active, concerned Black pastor in a multiplicity of directions every day, in addition to pastoral visits, hospital calls, family crises, etc. An appointment should be made to see the pastor and it should not be taken as a personal affront, if the appointment has to be made more than once. A call to the pastor's home early in the morning on the day of the appointment to reconfirm it, and a call again before going to keep it, may save some unnecessary frustration, anguish and time.

In smaller membership churches, the pastor will usually have full-time secular employment to provide for his/her family's income and support. Here again, the nature of the job dictates this as a necessity for most pastors. The pastor's family must operate in the economy of the community along with other families. Black congregations, made up primarily of women and children, have very limited finances with which to operate. What is called a pastor's salary is often less than a poor honorarium for the services rendered. In most instances, the income is below federal government's poverty level guidelines for a single person; it is hardly more than an income supplement for a family.

A worker with the elderly can become highly frustrated trying to reach a Black pastor who works a secular job, for there is no clerical person taking telephone messages or making appointments. Success in this environment requires a little imaginative thinking, and adjustment in the work schedule and dedication to the task.

Where the congregation meets every Sunday for worship, a contact can be made following the worship service. It would be somewhat intrusive to make contact with a pastor on Sunday before the church services. After the services have concluded, the pastor should be courteous enough to make arrangements for a conference, if he/she is unavailable for one at that time. Get telephone numbers for follow-up conversation and future contact—telephone numbers at home and on the job, if calls are receivable at work. The best time to reach any pastor at home is before eight o'clock in the morning and after ten o'clock in the evening.

If a congregation does not meet each Sunday for worship, parishioners at a nearby church should be able to provide helpful information which will lead to a contact with the pastor. They should be able to provide the pastor's name, where he/she lives, when the church holds services, the names of two or three lay members and how to contact them. One of these key lay workers should be able to provide a mailing address and residence telephone number for the pastor.

In rural areas some congregations still hold worship services one or two Sundays per month. However, they may hold Sunday School each Sunday. The Sunday School superintendent or a teacher may have the information needed for contacting the pastor. Sunday School is usually held between the hours of nine-thirty and eleven o'clock. This is a good time to make contact.

Until the pastor encourages contact with the members of his/her congregation and indicates who he/she deems to be the appropriate person(s) for the contact, it is best to withhold detailed information. It should be sufficient to note that the outside workers are consulting with pastors in the area on community outreach and community ministry. To share any more information may prove to be self-defeating in situations where some members work at having others think that they are more knowledgeable than the pastor.

The point is that one's approach to entry into a Black congregation will depend on how one understands the Black Church. One may put forth some effort to understand it and, thereby, find effective ways to enter its system and accomplish desired goals or one may blunder his/her way into it and hope for the best. An experienced or thoughtful worker with the elderly wants results and approaches any system only after some analysis of it. Those who would get results as liaison persons, enablers, recruiters or trainers with either clergy or laity of Black Churches must spend some time in careful preparation before taking the first step in their direction.

RECRUITING AND TRAINING IN THE BLACK CHURCH

Recruiting Black pastors for educational/training programs in gerontology is a major undertaking. It can be a very frustrating task. Denominational programs get their first consideration since many of the national bodies now include some learning experiences in their conventions, assemblies and convocations. Pastors can enjoy the fellowship of their co-workers while engaged in learning experiences with them. This is also true at the lower judicatory levels. State conventions, Episcopal Districts, Presbyteries, Annual Conferences, District Associations, etc., sponsor schools, seminars, worship, institutes for the pastors in the jurisdiction and put pressure on them to attend. Gerontology could be one of the topics included in such meetings.

Pastors working secular jobs have a limited number of days annually which they can take off and remain employed. They schedule some of their days for church related responsibilities and some for family and personal duties. The few Black pastors in a community who are full-time in the ministry are stretched to the limit and are, therefore, not likely to see another training session as a very high priority matter. Once a recruiter understands the reality and the odds he/she is facing, expectations can be set accordingly.

Since recruitment is selling a product, and since the competition for pastors' time is stiff, the recruiter must have an irresistible presentation. Both the content and the form of the presentation must be planned for maximum effect. Pastors are communicators. They are impressed with those who have mastered the art and may be persuaded by someone who has taken the time to put together a challenging presentation. Using the same logic, they may be turned off by someone who extends an invitation but has little more to offer, or by someone who has a program to offer but presents it poorly. They may well reason that if this is a sample, a foretaste of what will be offered, time cannot be wasted on that program.

Facts about the program are important to share, such as time commitment required, schedule, location, presenters, costs, accommodations, etc. These should be presented toward the end of the conversation, however. Pastors need to be confronted with their responsibility for ministry to and with the elderly in a way that is both exciting and challenging. They need facts about the elderly. Four or five provocative questions about the plight, the condition, the status of elderly Black people in the area, should get an interesting discussion going with a concerned pastor. The questions should lead to the sharing of little known information so that the pastor will have learned something, had his/her appetite stimulated, curiosity piqued and a desire raised to learn more of what the program has to offer. Questions such as: Have you any idea about the number or percent of the elderly Blacks in this state or county that live in poverty? Or how many or what percent in this county? What percent of poor elderly Black people would you guess have no knowledge of the medical benefits they are entitled to and, therefore, may have no medical insurance to cover them in the case of illness? What foods found in the diet of most Black Americans would you think are detrimental to the health of the elderly? What do you think elderly people can do to protect themselves against violence perpetrated against them by family members or by offenders when they are on the streets? How can a congregation organize itself to minister to problems of the elderly?

Such questions can begin to heighten a pastor's awareness to the fact that he/she may need to learn more about a significant segment of the congregation and the community. Missed opportunities for ministry may begin to flash through the pastor's mind and possibilities for future programming might be imagined. A concerned pastor will want more of what has been presented in a brief visit. A good worker will pique the pastor's interest and bring the presentation to a halt. Stop the presentation while the prospect's interest is high and then seek a commitment for participation. A person's skill is put to a real test at this point. The desired result is a participant in the training program dealing with Black elderly concerns.

In addition to training in seminaries, pastors should be encouraged to attend sessions on aging. They can visualize ministries operative in and through the church, and they have entree to other persons who may be interested in doing ministries to, with and by older members. Often the pastors will point to persons who are in place in their church system, the president of an auxiliary, chairperson of a board or circle, leader of a group. Such persons may be helpful but they may not be the ones with time or interest in training in gerontology. The pastor should be urged to think carefully about the recommendations for potential program participants.

Because the Black Church is predominantly female, most of the lay trainees recommended will be women. The women's division of the church usually does community outreach work. The circles adopt projects or create them to meet needs in the community. The men's groups tend to limit their service to work in the church rather than outside of the church. An alert worker will be intentional about seeking some males for the training program. If the pastor fails to name any men, ask if there are any who may be considered. Male lay prospects are often more difficult to recruit than are their pastors. Women in the congregation who will participate in the gerontological training can assist with recruiting their brothers in faith, if encouraged to do so. Most men appear to need familiar support around them for such endeavors. They are more likely to respond positively, if they know that other members of their church will be participating and if they know laymen from other churches who will be involved.

Lay volunteers for ministry to and with the elderly are usually middle-aged or older. Persons in these age groups have a natural stake in such ministries because they see themselves in need of such ministries in the not too distant future. Young adults and youth must be confronted with their responsibility to minister to elderly persons. A congregation in ministry to the elderly should be inclusive of all who can share in it. Black youth and young adults need the challenge to render service to the elderly. Some of their strength, energy and resources should be channeled to assist those who paved the way for them. Here again, the worker should provoke the pastor's thinking. What youth and what young adults can be considered? A resourceful leader from each group would help to broaden future program possibilities.

If it is to be relevant to leaders in the Black Church, if it is going to address the needs they are to confront with the Black elderly, the training programs must include a significant amount of information on the Black elderly. Some problems facing the elderly are common to all regardless of race or ethnic background. Some, however, focus upon the Black elderly disproportionately. Pastors in Black communities should be informed and knowledgeable about these conditions. The National Caucus and Center On The Black Aged has funded research studies which have revealed startling information on the plight of older Blacks in the areas of income, housing, health, nutrition, mental health, life expectancy, etc. Researchers on elderly Blacks (such as Jacquelyn Jackson, Forrest B. Tyler, Harold W. Neighbors, James S. Jackson, Linda M. Chatters and

Vira Kivett) have documented a wealth of information to take seriously the presence of Black elderly participants.

CONCLUSIONS

West Africa is Black America's homeland. The Black Church in America reflects that history in its worship and communal life. Consolidated in one figure of the Black pastor are the meanings and roles of the tribal chief, medicine man, witch doctor and tribal elder. Though these are cultural and historical traits now often unconsciously transmitted, the power of the reality is currently with us. Anyone who would work in or with the Black Church must put forth some effort to understand it. In its present form the pastor is pivotal. The growing, active, strong congregations have charismatic, eloquent, dramatic personalities in the pulpit. They draw, they attract, they pull the masses in their direction.

The people love the pastor for they sincerely believe that God has endowed him/her to lead them as the pastor is being led by the Divine power of God. Persons who wish to share ideas for ministry to, with and through the elderly with a congregation will experience greater success, if those ideas are shared with the pastor first. The pastor's sanction is important in most churches. If that sanction is not given, good ideas can be smothered by the pastor's indifference toward them.

The recruitment of Black pastors for training programs in gerontology requires unusual patience, perseverance and skill. Even more appears to be needed to involve Black laymen. In training lay volunteers for ministry with the elderly, youth and young adults should be targeted along with men. Middle-aged and elderly women carry the major work load for mission and ministry outside of the church. Others should be challenged and encouraged to join them.

Luther Northwestern Theological Seminary: Program in Aging

Melvin A. Kimble, PhD

SUMMARY. This is a description of one of the largest and most innovative programs in aging related to a seminary and included in this project. Begun in 1983, it has grown in faculty and student support. It takes advantage of Lutheran and ecumenical involvement. It has developed a working relationship with a state university.

Luther Northwestern Theological Seminary, through a series of mergers covering more than half a century, represents the consolidation into one seminary of what at one time were six separate institutions dating back to 1869. It is one of the eight seminaries of the Evangelical Lutheran Church in America and is located in the heart of the "Twin Cities," Minneapolis and St. Paul, a metropolitan area in excess of 2,000,000 persons and the center of the most Lutheran section of North America.

Luther Northwestern Theological Seminary is one of the five seminaries that make up the Minnesota Consortium of Theological Schools. Cross-registration for all courses, a joint Doctor of Ministry program, as well as extensive interlibrary cooperation, represent areas of collaboration by Bethel Theological Seminary (Baptist General Conference), Luther Northwestern Theological Seminary (Evangelical Lutheran Church in America), The School of Theology of St. John's University, Collegeville (Roman Catholic), The

Melvin A. Kimble is Professor of Pastoral Theology and Ministry and Director of the Program in Aging, Luther Northwestern Theological Seminary, Saint Paul, MN.

St. Paul School of Divinity (Roman Catholic), and United Theological Seminary of the Twin Cities (United Church of Christ). The schools serve a public that includes some 1,750 theological students, their graduates and immediate constituencies of clergy and lay persons, and the academic community of the region which includes two universities and seven colleges.

The academic work at Luther Northwestern Theological Seminary embraces five degree programs: Master of Divinity, Master of Arts, Master of Theology, Doctor of Ministry, and Doctor of Theology. All programs include the Program in Aging as a concentration or major. Luther Northwestern Theological Seminary is the largest Lutheran seminary in North America with a January, 1988 enrollment of 701 students.

Since almost nowhere else can Lutherans be found in such numbers and variety of ethnic backgrounds, the student has unexcelled opportunities for field work and ministry in the hundreds of Lutheran congregations. In addition, Luther Northwestern Theological Seminary has relationships with a variety of social service agencies, hospitals, hospices, geriatric and long-term centers which provide unique and extraordinary clinical contextual educational sites for hands-on ministry.

HISTORY OF THE DEVELOPMENT
OF THE PROGRAM IN AGING

The purpose of the Aging Program undertaken at Luther Northwestern Theological Seminary in June, 1983, was to promote the development of future ministers and lay professional leaders of the church who will be capable of addressing the needs of the elderly and developing support services for them by utilizing parish resources. The program was launched as a two-year research and demonstration project by a grant from the Retirement Research Foundation of Park Ridge, Illinois. Dr. Melvin Kimble served as Project Director and Dr. Michael Hendricksen served as Principal Investigator.

Within educational institutions generally, the level of commitment to a given subject is gauged by whether it is treated as an occasional topic within a course, whether it has reached a level of relative importance to be treated as an elective, or viewed as intrinsic to the basic preparation of professionals and deserving to be given the level of support as a concentration. In order for this to occur, an increasing need for training in unique skills and knowledge must be acknowledged and a model program developed and implemented within an educational setting. The purpose of this project was to create such a model for seminary students. Specifically, the project was to create and implement a ten-course concentration within the curriculum.

Due to the classical approach to theological education used by most faculty members at LNTS, there was a predisposition to view the Aging Program as a peripheral topic subsumed under existing pastoral care courses, rather than central to understanding of mission and ministry. The most effective effort in deepening understanding of and support for the program was a separate two-day conference held for the faculty and administration in the spring of the first year. The conference theme was "Perspectives in Aging" and included the following presentations from nationally known experts: "A Theologian's Role in the Field of Aging," Joseph Sittler, Emeritus Professor of Systematic Theology, University of Chicago; "Aging as a Scientific and Value Laden Field of Inquiry," James Birren, Executive Director and Dean, Andrus Gerontology Center, University of Southern California; "The Strategic Role of the Church and Its Future Mission in the Field of Aging," Michael Hendrickson, Associate Professor and Senior Research Scientist, USC; "Personal Perspectives on Aging," Gerhard Frost, Professor Emeritus of Practical Theology, Luther Northwestern Theological Seminary.

This panel of presenters stimulated faculty members to expand their perspective on aging and relate it more fully to their areas and disciplines of academic theological inquiry. The conference and subsequent discussions were pivotal opportunities to emphasize integrative aspects of this cross-disciplinary program that appropriately and vitally relates to courses in all disciplines of the seminary curriculum. Some of the results included a number of faculty volunteering to participate in courses in the Aging Program, as well as expressing their interest in incorporating aging issues within their own departmental courses during the next academic year. An Advisory Committee composed of faculty members from each of the five departments of the seminary, as well as student representatives, was established to provide input into the content of the program and to broaden understanding of its objectives.

Initial efforts during the first year focused on creating a strong clinical experiential learning component to the program. The establishment of a part-time position of Coordinator of Geriatric Clinical Experiences and staffing it with a semi-retired CPE chaplain and former Director of Chaplaincy for Minnesota Lutheran Social Services resulted in the identification and cultivation of a select group of geriatric chaplains and institutions to be utilized by the program. Two workshops were held with chaplains chosen to participate as clinical supervisors to introduce them more fully to the objectives of the program. A Clinical Advisory Council was established comprised of ten chaplains representing nursing homes, retirement communities, hospital and urban parish settings with large elderly populations.

COURSE CONTENT

The concentration includes 35 hours of course work lodged primarily within the Department of Pastoral Theology and Ministry. Several sections of core departmental courses were revised to provide a basic orientation towards aging and skills in counseling older adults. Additional courses were introduced to fulfill other objectives of the program: (1) a focus on the social-physiological-spiritual-ethical dimensions of aging and growing old; (2) the types of service programs which the church could develop and administer; and (3) the kinds of value-laden issues which an increasingly aging society brings forth.

Supervised on-site experiences in geriatric centers, hospices, parishes with aging memberships, and church-related social agencies are included as clinical components in every course. A quarter of Clinical Pastoral Education (480 hours) is offered in accredited geriatric centers under the direction of certified CPE chaplains. Internships are available for 12-month placements in congregations with elderly concentrations, hospitals, and long-term care geriatric settings.

Key to the aging program's growth and success was the expansion of the program beyond a departmental pastoral care specialty to a more interdisciplinary, interdepartmental one. This insured its position as a central element within the seminary's curriculum. Specific strategies were developed during the third and fourth years of the program to achieve this objective. One strategy was to design a required interdisciplinary Text and Context core elective course team taught by a senior member of the Old Testament Department and a senior member of the Pastoral Theology Department. This course, Biblical and Pastoral Perspectives on Aging, was first offered in 1985-86 and has continued to be popular with students. Plans are underway to offer several other interdisciplinary courses in conjunction with other departments.

There are currently 11 aging concentration courses: Ministry with the Aging, Pastoral Theology; Ministry to the Aged and the Bereaved; Basics of Pastoral Care and Counseling; Aging Section, Text and Context in Theology; Biblical and Pastoral Perspectives on Aging; The Church as a Primary Delivery System of Services for the Elderly; Aging Section, Clinical Pastoral Education; Medical Ethics in Theological Perspective; Death and Dying; Physiology and Health Promotion in the Later Years; and Guided Reading and Research.

DEGREE PROGRAMS

Initially, the Program in Aging focused on the Master of Divinity curriculum and the preparation of ordained clergy, but it soon targeted the Master of Arts program and the preparation of persons who are engaged, or plan to be engaged, in various lay ministries in the church (e.g., parish assistants, older adult ministry directors, chaplain assistants in long-term care centers, etc.). This allows an enlargement of the aging concentration option for the MA degree which involves a total of 72 hours.

From the very beginning of the program, graduate students in the Th.M. and D.Min. program were admitted to courses in the Aging Program. Innovative and scholarly dissertations and research projects have been produced by D.Min. graduates who have completed the concentration. Examples of dissertation topics are set forth in the following:

> 1984 – "The Importance of Being Important: Some Theological Reflections on the Self-Image of the Elderly" by Rev. Sigfinnur Thorleifsson (Icelandic Lutheran pastor).
>
> 1985 – "A Room Called Remember" by Rev. Robert Pearson (Lutheran parish pastor). A videotape designed to introduce life review as a method for mutual ministry.
>
> 1986 – "Psychological Development and Human Aging: An Empirical-Descriptive Approach" by Father David McPhee (Roman Catholic parish priest).
>
> 1987 – "A Pastoral Care Approach to Ministry with the Aging" by the Rev. Lloyd Mart (a Lutheran geriatric chaplain).

The academic year 1987-88 marked the introduction of a Th.D. program in Pastoral Care and Counseling with five concentrations: Aging, Youth and Family, Chemical Dependency, Family Counseling, and Diversified Counseling. This program holds promise of adding both scholarly depth and breadth to the Aging Program.

Presently, a joint-degree program in long-term care administration with North Texas State University, Denton, Texas, has been approved in principle by the faculty and Board of Directors and is currently taking final shape. This, too, will increase the scope of the Aging Program and provide additional options for students.

One of the by-products coming out of the Aging Program is *Bless Bible Studies*, for use as a spiritual care ministry to persons residing in health care centers and nursing homes. Bible study materials which are flexible for use on a monthly or weekly basis include four 12-session studies, each with a 48-page leader guide. This study along with a participant leaflet and an audiocassette tape of vocal and organ accompaniments are published by ELCA Publishing House, Augsburg/Fortress, Minneapolis, Minnesota. The team of authors for this material includes several who have been part of the Aging Program at Luther Northwestern Theological Seminary. They developed parts of this series as course work projects.

SPECIAL PROGRAMS

The Aging Program has scheduled regular community and seminary seminars and programs. For example, in 1985-86, a series of programs involved emeriti professors and their spouses in several evenings of sharing on specific topics of interest to the seminary community. During 1986-87, one of the events planned by the Aging Program was a Conference on Cross-Cultural Gerontology with Dr. Helen Kerschner, President and Executive Director, American Association for International Aging, Washington, D.C., and Dr. Helen Sotomayor, President and CEO, National Hispanic Council on Aging, Washington, D.C. This conference, which was made possible with the assistance of a grant from Aid Association for Lutherans, was designed to broaden awareness and understanding of cross-cultural aging issues, with special emphasis on the non-Western world. It included panelists from an assortment of countries represented in the student body and LNTS professors of Christian Missions and World Religions.

Continuing opportunities are available for pastors and lay professionals by the "Kairos" seminars which are week-long on-campus education programs scheduled throughout the academic year. Normally, the wide range of topics scheduled during the year include several offerings on aging issues.

An objective of the Aging Program was to be more involved in community education and networking within the St. Anthony Park neighborhood of the seminary. In the spring of 1987, planning began for a community education experiment on Ethics and Aging. With the assistance of an Award for Innovation from the Ford Foundation, the St. Anthony Park Block Nurse Program and Luther Northwestern Theological Seminary designed four programs on successive Monday evenings. They focused on ethical decision-making issues related to health and well-being of older persons who lived at home. In addition to case studies, presentations and panel discussions, informational material and a bibliography on the issues were handed out at each session. The programs are offered without cost and are open to all neighborhood residents.

The primary objectives are: (1) to assist people in the process of ethical reasoning in regard to issues related to the health and well-being of older persons, particularly as experienced in the home and community setting; (2) to convey to participants the realization that the authority for decision-making in areas of values and beliefs rests with the individual and his or her family and community. Secondary objectives include: (1) raising awareness of the need for support of individuals and families dealing with difficult situations and decisions in this area of concern, and (2) providing specific information where its lack is evident and good resources are available.

AGING PROGRAM LEADERSHIP

Leadership for the Aging Program is provided through a cadre of LNTS faculty, administration, and students. Dr. Melvin Kimble, Professor of Pastoral Theology and Ministry, has served as Director of the Aging Program since its introduction into the curriculum in 1983. In addition to the designated instructors for the courses cited, a number of LNTS faculty from all five departments participate in courses as lecturers and resource persons. Many courses in the program also avail themselves of some of the many gerontological educators and practitioners in the Twin Cities. The support of and commitment to the program by the Office of the President, the Dean of Academic Affairs, and the Director of Admissions, as well as by the Vice President for Seminary Relations have been crucial in making the Aging Program a permanent and significant interdisciplinary concentration in the curriculum.

FUTURE PLANS

Plans for the future include the implementation by September, 1988, of a joint M.A. degree program in Aging by Luther Northwestern Theological Seminary and North Texas State University, Denton, Texas, in conjunction with the Good Samaritan Society of Sioux Falls, South Dakota. The purpose of this joint program is to provide continuing education for administrators of nearly 400 nursing homes (including almost 200 Evangelical Lutheran Church in America long-term care facilities) across the country. The program is designed to combine biblical and theological study with the study of issues related especially to the administration of long-term health care facilities. The Aging Program at Luther Northwestern Theological Seminary and the Center for Studies in Aging at North Texas State University will direct the program on their respective campuses.

Other future plans for the Aging Program are to strengthen and solidify existing facets of the program, including the new Th.D. Aging concentration, and to develop new strategies for program promotion and student recruitment.

Nashotah House:
Gerontology and the Curriculum
at a Small Episcopal Seminary

Charles F. Caldwell, PhD

SUMMARY. This is the story of efforts to deal with aging concerns in a seminary with a small student body and a highly structured and required curriculum. This account may prove helpful to many seminaries facing similar situations.

Nashotah House is a small (about seventy students) seminary of the Episcopal Church, located in semirural Wisconsin about thirty-five miles west of Milwaukee. Students are engaged in pastoral, spiritual and academic formation within the Anglo-Catholic tradition. This formation process includes study, prayer, and work, which means that in addition to classes, students are expected to be in chapel daily and to do work-crew in the refectory or on the grounds weekly. Since Nashotah is a residential seminary with both married and single students living on campus, there is an intensive community life which is an important aspect of learning. The average age of our students is thirty-seven, so that our younger students live closely with older students who are entering second careers or even dealing creatively with retirement. After the first year, most students are also engaged in ministerial work in area parishes, where they experience some of the problems and opportunities of aging congregations.

If a small school such as Nashotah House offered special courses or seminars in all of the skills, concerns, interests, and issues

---

Charles F. Caldwell is Assistant Professor of Pastoral Theology, Nashotah House, Nashotah, WI.

needed in pastoral ministry and suggested by various groups, it seems there would be no time for the regular, basic curriculum. If we only taught the "nuts and bolts" of ministry, what we taught would likely be out-of-date before some of the students graduated. Therefore, we try to teach students to think theologically from a pastoral perspective of responsible concern for the proclamation of the gospel, the mission of the church in the world, the cure of souls and the worship of God. This is so that the minister might understand the word of God in a way which is true to the Scripture and Tradition of the Church and to human experience. We try to teach students to read the written documents of the tradition and the "living human documents" theologically. This basic orientation is evidenced by the book *Anglican Theology and Pastoral Care*, edited by our systematics professor, Fr. James Griffiss.

Nashotah House thinks of itself more as a professional school for ministry than as a vocational training or a graduate academic school. This means that there is a fairly fixed curriculum in which all the required and elective courses are oriented towards preparation for ministry.

Gerontological concerns may therefore be addressed in any course of study. Systematic Theology attempts to understand the gospel as addressed to the human condition in contemporary society and from year to year selects a variety of pastoral and social issues for special focus. While the content of these in-course workshops with outside speakers has not been specifically gerontological, they do set a pattern of thinking theologically about human experience which is transferable. In other disciplines, gerontological issues arise naturally in the course of study. In Ethics and Moral Theology the issues of abortion and euthanasia, for instance, raise questions about how we think of the very young and old, how people on the "edges of society" are treated, how we organize and make decisions socially. The primary approach is through the concerns of biomedical ethics, but the larger context is a concern of issues in contemporary society. How gerontological concerns are addressed in the various courses depends on the nature of the discipline and the awareness of the teacher, but the orientation of the school towards preparation of ministry inclines teachers to be aware of the parish situation in which there are significant numbers of older people. Liturgy is concerned with the sanctification of life, and out of this concern our Liturgics Professor, Fr. Louis Weil, has just written an article for AARP entitled "Liturgy and Aging."

The curriculum in pastoral theology at Nashotah House has been revised in the last three years, with the coming of a new dean and a new pastorals professor. Prior to 1985, during the interim period when there was no regular professor of pastoral theology, an elective course in gerontology was taught by the chaplain at a Milwaukee retirement/nursing home. It consisted of supervised ministry and readings. In order to make this offering more academically respectable, the seminary in 1985 made use of a continuing education course offered at a local retirement/nursing home. This course required supervised ministry in the home, workshops with doctors and nurses, lectures by a qualified gerontologist on site, and a written pastoral theological case study done under the supervision of the pastoral professor at the seminary. These courses did not have large enough markets in the seminary or among the local clergy and had to be dropped. As the Dean said upon his arrival, "No student should leave seminary without having set foot in a nursing home." Gerontological concerns should be an integral part of a pastorals curriculum, if students are to be prepared for the parish situations in which most of them will serve. Specialized ministries should be understood in terms of general ministry, and a pastorals curriculum should provide a way of integrating theory and practice, action and reflection, theology and experience. We did not want to divorce the academic and ministerial aspects of pastoral theology.

It was decided to rearrange the three year sequence of academic pastorals courses, so that introduction to pastoral counseling would be given in the junior year, introduction to pastoral theology in the middler year, and introduction to pastoral ministry in the senior year. The counseling course could thus serve as a preparation for clinical pastoral education (C.P.E.), which is usually taken in the summer after the first year, and the Pastoral Theology course could serve as a follow-up for C.P.E. An attempt was made to introduce a field education component to each of these courses. While this has been successful for the first two courses, it had to be dropped from the senior course. But the seniors already had a week-long special seminar given by the Tri-Diocesan Commission on Alcoholism and

Other Drug Abuse. This required offering was expanded to include a series of workshops with visiting instructors on a variety of practical topics.

Gerontological issues arise naturally in each of the three pastorals courses. In the counseling course, students are asked to understand the individual life story as part of the story of mankind as told in the Bible. They are asked to consider several psychological points of view, including those of Freud, Jung, and Augustine. And so they are invited to look at the human life cycle and stages of personal development in different ways during the course. This prepares them not only for C.P.E. but also for Christian Education and Homiletics. Among the required readings is Erikson's "Eight Ages of Man." Most of our students in the junior year are not yet ready to take on serious counseling cases, but they need to be intentionally engaged in the field with what is being discussed in class. They are asked to call in local nursing/retirement homes, to enter relationships with caring concern and to practice the skills of listening and responding with attention to human dynamics. For most students an important part of this field education component is hearing the stories and appreciating the experience of older people. The focus in the practical component of the course is not so much on field work as on field education, not so much on doing ministry with older people as on understanding the human condition and listening to people as a first step in ministry.

After a summer of C.P.E. the student takes the middler course in pastoral theology. Various methods of doing pastoral theology are reviewed, including the "practical theology" of Karl Rahner, the "liberation theology" of Juan Luis Segundo, the "pastoral theology" of Seward Hiltner, and the "applied theology" of Martin Thornton. Students are asked to do a case study in which they interpret the word of God in a way which is true to the written documents of the tradition and true for the experience of the "living human documents" of the pastoral case. In discussing the hermeneutic issues involved, we read an article by Karl Rahner, "The Sacrifice of the Mass and an Ascesis for Youth," which discusses the different meanings the word "sacrifice" might have in the experience of younger, middle-aged, and older people. The "life cycle" concerns of the counseling course are perhaps reinforced by being discussed in a new context. Gerontological issues are related to other issues from a pastoral perspective.

The field work component of the middler course provides an opportunity for a more specialized gerontological focus. Students are asked to do two hours' work a week in a field placement which involves supervised ministry and provides readings and instruction for that ministry. Through the cooperation of the Bishop of Milwaukee we have been able to obtain placements with supervisors who also do work for Marquette University. Students work with prisoners, the hungry, the homeless, battered women, the developmentally disabled, and the aged. The chaplain at St. John's Home has been enthusiastic about providing an experientially based minicourse in gerontology. He provides a bibliography for reading in gerontology, as well as supervising practical ministry. St. John's has a retirement home, a nursing home, a home visitation program, and a number of activities which involve people of various ages. While not all of our students can participate in all of the placements, the community at Nashotah is close enough that students learn from one another. As a final requirement for the middler course students are asked to write a pastoral theological case study on either their C.P.E. experience or their field education experience.

In the second trimester of the middler year, students have a full-time "hands-on" experience of ministry through the Teaching Parishes Program (TPP). They serve under the direction of a pastor in selected parishes around the country. In the third trimester there is a one hour a week TPP seminar for which students are asked to write a case study based on their TPP experience and to use the writing of the case study as a basis for sharing their experience and theological reflection in the seminar group. Through this TPP program many students get to see firsthand the proportion of older people in congregations, how ministry is done with the elderly, and how retirees can serve as volunteers in the church and the community. In particular, students who go to certain parishes in Florida can see that older people are not all in nursing or retirement homes, and that congregations with a preponderance of older people can be lively, generative, and mission minded. This experience is shared in the seminars, through community life, and in the Homiletics class.

In the second trimester of the senior year there is a series of workshops and seminars given by people active in various practical fields. There is always a week-long workshop on alcoholism and other drug abuse which, coming toward the end of the curriculum, is usually an event of personal and practical insight. And every year there is a seminar on Canon Law. In addition we have had seminars/ workshops in stewardship, evangelism, church growth, and parish administration. The topics are variable, so that we can respond to the felt needs of the church and seminary. In the two years this series has been offered, we have not had a seminar/workshop in gerontology, because of the field education minicourse at St. John's Home. The chaplain at the Home is ready and able to provide leadership in this area.

The course, "Introduction to Pastoral Ministry," is offered in the third trimester of the senior year. It looks at ministry under the headings of the proclamation of the gospel, the mission of the church in the world, the cure of souls, and the worship of God, with parish administration as a subheading. Whereas the counseling course was psychologically oriented, the ministry course is sociologically oriented. Gerontological concerns arise as we look at social statistics and the aging of the population in the nation and the church. Ministry to and with older people is also directly considered when we discuss the ministry of the pastor.

A final course in liturgy is required of seniors at the same time they are taking the final course in ministry. The liturgics course covers the history, theology and administration of the sacraments. The ministry course deals with pastoral issues in church and society which may be understood through a consideration of the pastoral significance of the sacraments. In this way, a concern for the sanctification of life and the pastoral care of the aging can reinforce each other.

Of course, gerontological concerns come up in the classroom as professors use examples drawn from experience to illustrate a theological understanding of our human condition. The use of such illustrations may arise naturally in an institution oriented towards theological preparation for ministry, where most of our students will go into the parish. This will depend on the awareness of the individual professor. Projects and events which focus that awareness in specific as well as general ways help keep the seminary responsive to the changing face of the church and society. Conferences and information sharing with those who study gerontology help keep a fairly fixed curriculum lively. Seminaries with modest resources need the help and the resources of larger institutions with gerontology programs.

Pittsburgh Theological Seminary:
A Project in Gerontology

Edward A. Powers, PhD
Thomas B. Robb, PhD
Susan N. Dunfee, PhD

SUMMARY. An account of what happens when a part-time consultant in gerontology is assigned the task of introducing aging-related programs into a seminary. The involvement of the denomination makes this a special case. The future results of this model are uncertain.

Pittsburgh Theological Seminary is a graduate professional institution of the Presbyterian Church (U.S.A.). The Seminary offers three theological degrees (Master of Divinity, Master of Arts, Doctor of Ministry) and eight degrees jointly with the University of Pittsburgh, including Doctor of Philosophy, Master of Divinity/Master of Social Work, and Master of Divinity/Juris Doctor. There currently are 343 students: 194 in various Masters programs, 42 in the PhD program, and 107 Doctor of Ministry students.

One of the joint degree programs at the Seminary is the Master of Divinity/Master of Social Work degree offered in cooperation with the University of Pittsburgh Graduate School of Social Work. This joint effort enables students to receive both degrees in four years of post-baccalaureate work instead of the usual five years. One concentration in the joint program is gerontology. Other seminary stu-

Edward A. Powers is Visiting Professor of Ministry with Older Adults, Pittsburgh Theological Seminary, and Associate Dean, School of Human Environmental Sciences, University of North Carolina at Greensboro. Thomas B. Robb is Director, Presbyterian Office on Aging (U.S.A.). Susan N. Dunfee is Assistant Professor of Theology, Pittsburgh Theological Seminary.

dents not in the joint program can also enroll in gerontology courses offered by the University of Pittsburgh.

HISTORY OF AGING-RELATED OFFERINGS

In 1984 the Seminary entered into a cooperative agreement with the Presbyterian Office on Aging and the Pittsburgh Presbytery, both units of the Presbyterian Church (U.S.A.). The purpose was to demonstrate how Presbyterian theological seminaries can better equip ministers and Church educators for ministry with older adults. The project was not proposed by the faculty, but instead, was brought to the faculty as a project in which the Seminary would be involved. The Presbytery and the Office on Aging each provided financial support for the project while the Seminary provided in-kind support.

This approach to increasing aging-related information in seminary is fairly unique. Typically aging programs are developed when one or more of the existing faculty becomes interested in aging and therefore develops an aging emphasis, or when funds become available, often through an endowment, to hire new faculty to start an aging emphasis. In this project a temporary, part-time program consultant was appointed to work with the faculty. Powers, the first author of this paper was the consultant.

Activities that were to be initiated at the Seminary during this three-year project include:

a. appointing a part-time program consultant who will assist the faculty to:

   1. to increase their understanding of aging and older people,
   2. modify existing courses as needed to reflect awareness of older people and their needs,
   3. develop new courses on aging and ministry with other people, if needed,
   4. develop linkage with university gerontology programs in the Pittsburgh area,
   5. develop field education, internship and Doctor of Ministry project opportunities and placements involving ministry with older adults,

6. develop continuing education offerings on aging and ministry with older people;

b. co-hosting a colloquium at the end of this project for faculty from other Presbyterian seminaries;

c. seeking to continue, after funding ceases, the courses and programs developed under this project.

Factors both internal and external to the Seminary lead to this cooperative arrangement. There always has been some degree of interest in aging-related programming at the Seminary. Historically, aging information occasionally has been included as part of a few regular courses, principally in ethics, religious education, and pastoral care. Workshops and conferences on aging also were periodically offered at the Seminary.

At the same time there has been increasing concern within the denomination for the needs of older adults and the rapid "graying" of congregations. This has, in part, been prompted by the fact that at least half of all Presbyterians currently are over 50 years of age; one in five are 65 or older. A number of position papers and overtures on aging-related issues have been presented at recent General Assembly meetings, one of them resulting in the establishment of the Office on Aging in 1981.

The aging of the Church has been especially evident in southwestern Pennsylvania, an area of the country with a disproportionately high percentage of older adults. In the early 1980s, Pittsburgh Presbytery, a regional Church governing body, appointed an Associate Executive Presbyter whose sole responsibility was aging programming. The responsibility of this position has broadened somewhat in subsequent years, but aging programming is still a major component of the responsibility. A Subdivision on Aging has been established at the Presbytery level and has organized a number of aging programs within the area. This committee of the Presbytery has also encouraged increased aging activities at the Seminary with the hope that these would result in better trained pastors for local congregations.

COURSES AND SPECIAL PROGRAMS

During this three-year project, single lectures on aging were presented in one of the first courses taken by new students and a gerontology module has been added to the initial course in pastoral care. Two courses entirely on aging have been developed. The first, "The Crisis of Aging and the Church," has been offered by the first author of this report. The second, "Theology of Aging," was team-taught by the first and third authors. In this latter course, faculty at the Seminary were invited to discuss aging from the perspective of their disciplines.

Increasingly, Doctor of Ministry students are doing work in aging. One course on aging has been offered for them. Four Doctor of Ministry dissertations on aging-related topics have been submitted in the last two years.

Jerry D. Harrah, *Ministry To, With and For the Elderly*

Harper R. Edwards, *Developing a Widow's Support Group in Washington, PA*

Ronnie Moore, *The Church Meets the Needs of the Elderly Within the Congregation and Its Community*

Raymond M. Touvell, *Project for Evaluating How Well Mulberry Presbyterian Church is Fulfilling Her Ministry By, With and For Older Adults*

Special Programs

There have been a number of special offerings on aging during the three years of this project. Two continuing education courses on "You and Your Aging Parent" were offered during the first year. The aging of the Church was one of the themes at the summer School of Religion, a week-long continuing education program with nearly 100 pastors in attendance. The second year the Seminary hosted an aging conference, "The New Old: Ministry with the Aging Today" at which Maggie Kuhn, National Governor of the Gray Panthers, was the major presenter. The third year the Seminary hosted a working conference for representatives of all Presbyterian theological schools.

Leadership

Under the terms of the cooperative agreement, leadership for this demonstration project has been provided by a part-time program consultant. The amount of time the program consultant spent at the Seminary varied from an entire term one year to a series of short term visits another year. While at the Seminary he taught courses, conducted continuing education experiences, consulted with faculty, and met with students. There has been no formal training in gerontology for Seminary faculty. Although several seminars on aging were conducted with faculty, the increase in an understanding of aging and older adults has been facilitated by: (1) sharing papers, articles, and books with faculty, (2) discussions, and (3) the involvement of faculty in the team-taught course.

Field Education

Considering the changing demographics of western Pennsylvania and surrounding areas, most field education assignments for students will involve working with older adults. A number of the field education placements are in congregations in which a large majority of members are older. In addition, there currently are seven students whose field education is an aging assignment: one is working in a comprehensive senior center, two have been assigned to aging ministries by their supervisor and four are working on special projects in aging ministries with the Presbytery Subdivision on Aging.

DENOMINATIONAL POLICY AND PROGRAMMING

As early as 1717, the Presbyterian Church focused on the needs of older adults by establishing a fund to provide care for the widows of ministers. Since 1973, policy papers adopted by the Church's General Assembly have called for the development of ministers who encourage the spiritual growth and continued discipleship of older adults and respond to their needs and concerns. Attention has also been focused on public policies that affect the well-being of older adults.

In 1981, the Church established an Office on Aging as part of its national program agencies. This office has developed a wide range of program resources for congregations and initiated a series of training programs for pastors and lay leaders. In 1987, the General Assembly designated the continuing development of older adult ministries "an urgent priority" of the Presbyterian Church and authorized a three-year study to develop priorities and strategies for meeting this concern.

The current objectives of the denominational Office on Aging include:

1. nurture spiritual growth throughout each person's life;
2. reach out to those isolated by illness, frailty or loss through death;
3. enable older people to share their faith and commitment with others;
4. provide care and support during times of transition and personal distress;
5. encourage older adults' participation in the Church's mission and outreach;
6. bring about better understanding and awareness of aging and older people.

STUDENT TRAINING IN AGING

Nearly all students have experience with older adults in their field education assignments. Recently most students in the junior and middle years have received some instruction in aging through a lecture or module on aging in several required courses. To date, a minority have received extensive course-work in aging. For example, 25 students were enrolled in the Theology of Aging course. In general, it would appear that these students have been most interested in and benefited most from this project.

FUTURE PLANS AND DISCUSSION

The intent of this project was to increase faculty understanding of aging and to help introduce programs that will assist in the education of pastors. It will be up to the Seminary to continue the programs after the completion of the project.

There were six major goals which the program consultant was to address during this project. This is a review of some progress toward them.

1. Increase faculty understanding of aging and older people — several presentations on aging will have been given to the faculty by the completion of this project. Modules and lectures on aging were given in the classes of several professors and one class on aging has been team-taught. However, this goal was best achieved through the sharing of articles and books and in informal discussions that occurred over the three years.

2. Help faculty modify existing courses, as needed. Aging will be included in the required pastoral care course. Aging already is discussed in ethics courses and religious education courses, but a great deal more needs to be done. It was hoped that based on the three-year project faculty would incorporate aging issues and perspectives into the teaching of their various disciplines. This goal has been only modestly achieved because many faculty have not really assumed "ownership" of the project. As noted earlier, the project was not initiated by the faculty of the Seminary. While the faculty were supportive they did not always see how aging content should or could fit into the existing program. More energy should have been invested in educating the faculty about aging and an attempt made to involve more of the faculty in planning and project activities either before the project began or during the initial year.

3. Develop new courses. Two new courses were developed and taught. These courses, however, were either taught or team-taught by the first author of this paper who, as a temporary part-time consultant, is no longer on staff. Whether these will continue to be taught is uncertain. The team teacher of one of the courses is still on the faculty. She likely will propose a course in which aging is only one of the concerns. This course will focus on all of the major transitions in the human life span, of which aging is one.

4. Develop linkages with university gerontology program. The linkage with a social work program that offers courses and a concentration in aging already is in place.

5. Develop field education and Doctor of Ministry project opportunities. A number of students currently have field education placements in settings with large numbers of older adults and/or aging

ministry programs. There has been an increase in the number of Doctor of Ministry projects on aging-related issues.

6. Develop continuing education offerings on aging. There have been a number of aging programs the last three years.

The goals of this project were for the most part achieved, certainly as much as could be expected in three years with only a part-time consultant. The question now is whether the accomplishments will be maintained after the project terminates. Here we are less positive.

Ideally there should have been some organizational change that was a consequence of this project, i.e., a tenured-track faculty position created for gerontology, budget adjustments, or formalized programs. These have not occurred.

Equally important would be to have one or more permanent faculty who consider aging to be an area of emphasis. But, throughout this project the program consultant was identified as "the gerontologist" at the Seminary. Others would join in discussions, but ultimately he was the one to whom faculty and administrators turned if someone was to speak to the aging dimensions of any issue. A number of permanent faculty increased their understanding of aging and one or two are now "interested" in aging, but none currently declares aging as an area of concentration. If there is to be some permanence to the program developed in this project, one or more faculty are going to have to identify with the aging field; they are going to have to "advocate for aging" at the Seminary. In discussions of curriculum development someone must continue to stress the importance of course content on aging. As continuing education programs and field education sites are being identified, opportunities to learn more about older adults should be provided. And at least one person needs to be familiar with the aging literature so that new materials on aging and religion can be brought to the attention of the rest of the faculty. We are not convinced such an individual has or will emerge in the permanent faculty.

Thus we are not sure how permanent the programs are that have been initiated in this project. It will take several years to determine what permanent effect we have had.

Presbyterian School of Christian Education: Center on Aging

Henry C. Simmons, PhD

SUMMARY. This account describes ministry to, with and for older adults from the perspectives of religious education. The emphases are on teaching, research and resourcing. Contrasts and similarities are drawn between training for clergy and for religious educators in relation to older adults.

The Presbyterian School of Christian Education is a graduate theological school of the Presbyterian Church (U.S.A.). "The purpose of the Presbyterian School of Christian Education is to prepare men and women for service in Christian vocations with emphasis upon the educational work of the church at home and abroad" (Mission Statement). Thus, unlike seminaries that (within a Christian context) educate persons primarily for professional ministry of word, sacrament, and pastoral care, the School intentionally prepares women and men for work as professional Christian educators in various contexts (congregational, denominational, academic, etc.).[1] The School's basic degree is the Master of Arts in Christian Education; its advanced degree is the Doctor of Education. The average enrollment in the years 1983-1988 was 111 including about 15% international students from a dozen countries. The School is accredited by the Association of Theological Schools in the United States and Canada and the Southern Association of Colleges and Schools.

Henry C. Simmons is Professor of Religion and Aging and Director, Center on Aging, Presbyterian School of Christian Education, Richmond, VA.

75

This informal essay will first review the history of the School's attention to ministry with older adults; then it will inquire about the particular focus which arises when primary attention is given to preparation for the educational ministry of the Church.

A SENSE OF VISION

In the academic year 1973-74, the first course on aging, "Ministry to the Aging," was offered at PSCE. In 1978 a Center on Aging was founded in part with a substantial gift from the "Women of the Church Birthday Gift," in response to a perceived need at the School and in the denomination for special attention to older adults in the Church. What was the vision and the sense of promise which surrounded the founding and funding of the Center on Aging? A study of the correspondence and funding proposals of Kenneth Orr, then the President of PSCE, makes clear some of his initial assumptions: (1) the denomination is aging faster than the population at large; (2) concern for the aging is diminishing to the point that many older adults no longer feel integrally part of the whole community; (3) the Church has a remarkable opportunity to assist and educate its members in the vitally needed area of more effective ministry with the aging; (4) the Church is ready to be mobilized; (5) a fruitful ministry can result from creative and systematic planning which brings together the proclamation of the gospel and the insights of gerontology. Lastly, Dr. Orr proposed that for the personal religious formation and spiritual well-being of theological students and faculty, there should be regular opportunities for intergenerational learning and sharing. Within the theological community older adults should contribute to and benefit from worship, theological discussion, and the pursuit of truth.[2]

Whatever allowance we might make for the rhetoric of funding proposals, the fact is that people believed in the vision enough to commit substantial monies to the project and to commit the resources of the School to the founding of a Center on Aging to make real this quite remarkable vision. It is also worthy of note that these proposals were written and funded before Project-GIST (Gerontology In Seminary Training) brought the concern for older adults to the attention of theological schools.

FIRST INITIATIVES

From its beginning, the Center on Aging had three emphases: Teaching, research, and resourcing, thus demonstrating an integral relationship to the School's purpose. Over the years, the relative importance accorded each of these three emphases varied. In the first years of the Center, Dr. Albert Dimmock, a Presbyterian of wide pastoral experience with a doctorate from North Carolina State University in adult education and gerontology, set up a "Learning Resources Laboratory" as a major resource for the Church and the community. Its design relied heavily on self-directed, independent learning.

> The Learning Resources Laboratory invites students as adults to dig into their own problems, seeking knowledge and gaining skills in research to learn what happens to persons as they grow older, what are some of the particular crises they may expect to meet, and how to communicate with and support older persons in ways that will enhance the quality of life in their later years.[3]

The Director of the Center, serving as a consultant, was also available to assist local Church committees or individuals in finding help for particular questions, programs, or needs. In this, as in every aspect of the project, Dr. Dimmock was indefatigable. In the early years, much of the use of the learning resource center was by individuals and small groups from the Churches; in the later years of his tenure the highest level of use of the learning resource center was in conjunction with continuing education events which worked with teams from local Churches and judicatories.

The second major emphasis of the Center was research. This emphasis received more attention in the early 1980s when grants were won for research. Major projects included (1) the design, testing, and comparison of six models to enhance spiritual growth and development; (2) the development of a model to link older adults with specific needs to other older adults with resources; (3) the development of a preretirement program for Church professionals; (4) the design and testing of an instrument to aid Churches in discovering the support needs of their older people and in developing programming to meet these needs.

The third emphasis of the Center was teaching, within the regular curriculum of the School and in continuing education events. The courses within the School's curriculum were two: "Understanding Older Adults" and "Methods in Ministry with Older Adults." Although Dr. Dimmock was deeply interested in preparing students for ministry with older adults, this ordering — resourcing, research, and teaching — represented the priorities of the Director and the Advisory Council (a small group of advisors with professional connections to various national networks).

EMPHASIS ON "AGING"
IN THE CURRICULUM

When Dr. Dimmock retired in 1985, the faculty search committee and the Advisory Council chose to stress the importance of preparing the PSCE students for ministry with older adults. The School selected Henry Simmons as successor. A scholar who holds a doctorate in Psychology and Religion from the University of Ottawa, he had been a full-time faculty member in theological institutions since 1970, with responsibilities primarily in Christian Education from the perspective of human development at the master's and doctoral levels. His first published article in the area of aging gives clue to his orientation.[4] It identified some crucial religious needs in the inner, subjective life of aging persons, as these are shaped within a cultural context which largely ignores the old.

It was hoped by the faculty search committee and the Advisory Council that Dr. Simmons would bring the study of ministry with older adults more centrally into the curriculum. With this in mind, he developed and offered a series of courses: "Ministry with Older Adults," "Aging as a Spiritual Journey," "Aging and Ministry in America: History and Implications" (with Dr. James Smylie of Union Seminary), "Issues in Aging from Novels and Films," "Ethical Issues in Aging" (with Dr. Isabel Rogers of PSCE), "The Quest of the Spirit: Adult and Older Adult Years," and "Curriculum Development for Older Adults and Intergenerational Groups."

Although there is in process a thorough-going curriculum study, courses on ministry with older adults currently are not part of the core curriculum of PSCE and thus are not required. Over the years a relatively small percentage of students (about 35%) have taken courses in this area. The general American culture tends to make aging into the problem of the elderly which denies them basic human solidarity. This tendency is mirrored in the curricula of most theological institutions. In order to awaken a sense of the issues and to give the students a wider exposure to the Professor of Religion and Aging, Dr. Simmons was also invited to teach in alternating years one course required of most Master's students, "Aspects of Growth and Development," and one required of most doctoral students, "Seminar in Human Development." It is yet to be seen whether or not this will attract more students to courses specifically on educational ministry with older adults.

The focus of the resource center has shifted slightly to reflect a renewed sense of the importance of the preparation of its students (and others) for the educational ministry of the Church with older adults. In its earlier years, the resource center had been able to purchase widely—indeed almost comprehensively—in theoretical and applied gerontology. In more recent years it became clear that this would no longer be possible (for reasons of budget and space, given the extraordinary proliferation of resources in the field) nor desirable (given a more sharply focused curricular emphasis).

At a meeting of the Advisory Council in early 1987, a meeting attended by the Dean of Faculty and members who had helped shape the direction of the Center since its beginning, a decision was made to purchase comprehensively (and retrospectively as needed) in the areas of religion and aging, including ethics and aging, and in aging from the perspective of the humanities. Works in other areas of applied and theoretical gerontology would be purchased more selectively.

Some of the functions of the resource center are similar to the functions of the library of a theological institution, namely, to collect archival, research, and applied materials which support the mission or purpose of the institution, namely to prepare students to engage in the practice of ministry today. However, the situation of PSCE is somewhat different from that of most seminary libraries for several reasons.

1. There is one central library for the three schools that constitute the Richmond Theological Center.[5] The wide variety of curricular emphases in the three schools precludes the focused and thorough collection in the area of educational ministry with older adults that is necessary to fulfill the Center's task at PSCE.

2. The resource center is used by theological students and by a wider constituency. It is important that there be a skilled staff person available to assist those who come to study and learn.

3. The process of collecting materials which are suitable for preparing students and others for the practice of ministry with older adults is painstaking and time-consuming. The vast majority of materials that appear on aging are written within a "scientific" framework. While some of these are important for PSCE's purposes, they are usually readily available from other libraries in the Richmond area. Particularly in recent years the focus of the collection has been, as already noted, within the humanities in general, with special emphasis on works which are of help in studying the cultural, social, and religious worlds of the older adult. The selection and processing of materials, as well as the interpretation of these materials to those who come to learn, requires a full-time staff person (as well as some part-time student assistants) and warrants a resource center separate from the central library.

A "grace note" of the collection is a special section of novels, poems, plays, children's stories, and autobiographies. This part of the collection numbers about 100 volumes, and is an extraordinary resource for helping our students (whose average age is about 30) enter imaginatively into the world of the older adult.

The resourcing function of the Center on Aging has always included consultations. In the past two years, the Director of the Center has concentrated particularly on helping other theological institutions to explore ways in which they might introduce or strengthen an emphasis on ministry with the aging in their curricula. Some of this consulting has been in conjunction with the Association of Gerontology in Higher Education, some has been through several projects of the American Association of Retired Persons. All of it has been supported by PSCE as part of its contribution to a wider theological community.

RESEARCH

Research is the third function of the Center on Aging. During Dr. Dimmock's years, research was conducted on various program and model ministries with older adults in the Church. Much of this material is still available and useful; indeed the present Director relies heavily on it. Current field research, however, focuses on the religious history and present needs of, specifically, Richmond area Presbyterians. A model of research has been developed in which groups of three or four men or women of the same birth cohort discuss together with the researcher and a senior student "the way things were," in a series of interviews which are recorded and transcribed for study. Each interview session lasts about 90 minutes. In the first interview, the focus is on the participants at age 12, in the second at age 24, in the third at age 36, and so forth by twelves until the present day. The participants are drawn from similar Church circles. This tends to keep relatively constant the variables of class and ethnicity, and allows a study of the effect of gender and birth cohort on the development of religious, ethical, and social attitudes. This informs wider research on the religious life and religious education of older adults. But the reader will also note that this is already a type of religious education for the participants in which the curriculum is formed from their own lives.

RELATIONSHIP WITH THE DENOMINATION

The decision on the part of PSCE to relate the Center on Aging more clearly to the general curriculum of the School represented a judgement that the best service it could provide for the Church was the preparation of persons for educational ministry who were competent in the area of ministry with the aging. It certainly did not represent any lessening of commitment to the Church. Rather, it took into account the existence, since 1979, of the Presbyterian Office on Aging in Atlanta. This Office was not in existence when the Center on Aging was founded. The goals of the Office on Aging include: (1) the development and publication of program resources; (2) the training and support of skilled leaders (or "enablers"); (3) the development of support and information networks; (4) advocacy; (5) liaison with ecumenical and interfaith groups.

The relationship between the Office on Aging and the Center on Aging gradually grew clearer. The Director of each sat ex-officio on the Advisory Council of the other. And as the goals of PSCE's Center on Aging grew more sharply focused there was seen to be little overlap. In fact, it became increasingly clear that there was more to be done than both the Office and the Center could handle.

In the course of the reorganization which occurred in the union of the former United Presbyterian Church and the Presbyterian Church (U.S.A.) a decision was taken to phase out the Office on Aging by the end of 1989, thus institutionalizing in yet another way the marginalization of older adults by the society. How — and whether — the denomination will fulfill the function of the former Office on Aging and what this might imply for the Center on Aging at PSCE is unclear.

DISTINCTIVENESS OF AN EDUCATIONAL FOCUS

As was noted, the mission of PSCE is to prepare men and women for service in Church vocations with emphasis upon the educational work of the Church. Seminaries, in contrast, primarily educate persons for professional ministry of word, sacrament, and pastoral care. However, preparation for the educational ministry of the Church is not only the work of an institution like PSCE; virtually all Master of Divinity programs include courses in religious education, and many seminaries also offer formal degree programs in religious education. But it is the assumption of this essay that in most seminaries in the preparation of the pastor for ministry with older adults the dominant focus and model are those of pastoral care rather than education. The present inquiry may encourage some to balance a preparation for the pastoral care of the old with preparation for religious education of the old.

It should be noted that there is a wide range of issues to be addressed educationally and not simply at the level of pastoral care. This was articulated in a proposal which shaped the formation of the program at PSCE. In 1975 Josephine Newbury, retired Director of the Demonstration Kindergarten, studied the options which PSCE faced in extending and enriching its ministry with older adults. She wrote (in part):

> In addition to the clinically oriented course, [students need] an overview course [which] should include a consideration of the Judeo/Christian heritage of age and aging, analyzing our Biblical heritage on the value of the person, with special emphasis on aging. Attention should be given to contrasting this rich heritage to the conflicting values western society has placed on aging and how even the Christian has assimilated the values of our youth-oriented society often at the expense of our biblical heritage.[6]

There are at least two levels at which the educational ministry of the Church is called to address needs: at the level of the intergenerational Church congregation and at the level of those who are themselves older adults. At the first level, educators need to be prepared to work with their congregations in many areas including but not limited to: (1) education for an understanding of what it means to grow old in our culture; (2) an understanding of what the Scriptures and a particular Church tradition have to say about the realities of aging, old age, and death; (3) the responsibilities of the whole congregation to include all its members in worship and mission; (4) advocacy for the vulnerable old; (5) understanding and addressing the particular needs of older people in a variety of settings; (6) religious institutions and the social service system; (7) intergenerational relationships; (8) specific issues of relationships between adult children and aging parents; (9) transitions, death and bereavement; (10) hospice and respite care; (11) ethical issues and aging.

The Church is in a unique position to educate as a part of its mission. There is no other social institution which has such a large membership which gathers on a regular, intergenerational basis and theologically affirms the value of all persons. If students are to be prepared to exercise educational leadership in Churches, the curriculum of the theological institution must be oriented to the design and implementation of educational programs. This is important in education for ministry as there is little existing curricular material available for use in the Church. Educators and pastors who undertake this kind of education need to be prepared to be pioneers. Eventually, it is hoped, religious education practitioners will be supported in their efforts and themselves educated by materials and programs that reflect authentically the world of all people and educate for the whole of life and death. Such resources do not exist today.

At the level of those who are themselves "older adults" there are specific educational needs which the curriculum of the theological institution should address if it is successfully to prepare men and women for the practice of educational ministry. This essay identified three to be discussed within the perspective of religious education.

1. Programs of education for leisure and retirement will have to go beyond mere financial planning seminars or lessons in nutrition, exercise, volunteerism, and good health care as important as all these may be. Religious education must help learners come to an understanding of leisure which is consonant with religious traditions. These have related leisure to the pursuit of wisdom, the development of a life of prayer, study, avocations, the development of relationships, the pursuit of culture and the pursuit of justice and peace.

2. Programs of education for diminishment and loss must take into account that in old age the probability of loss (and the possibility of gain) increases. Mass American middle-class cultural value-systems provide no religiously worthwhile education for dealing with diminishment and loss. Indeed the culture is profoundly silent about the harsher aspects of old age and the threat of annihilation in death. It is the work of the educator to help people shape together a common understanding and voice about these vitally human issues.

3. Religious education necessarily deals with issues of personal meaning. Programs for social and theological critique are clearly within the province of religious education. Older adults must find meanings other than those assigned by a culture which marginalizes them through negative and dependent stereotypes. It is important that older adults cease to be victims of the various meanings of

growing old which the culture provides and learn to create life designs that can be rich and full of meaning — that is, religious.

A final aspect of the distinctiveness of an educational focus in preparation of men and women for ministry with older adults concerns the difference in style of the interaction between educator and older adult and pastor and older adult. In a pastoral care situation the one ministering speaks authoritatively, that is, speaks with the authority of the religious tradition. In a privileged one-to-one situation, a word of comfort, of forgiveness, of challenge is spoken. In the religious education of older adults, the goals of education are best served when the educator enables or facilitates growth towards understandings which have not yet been fully articulated. Older adults need to learn with each other what it is to be authentic older adults, and what it requires to transform existing cultural forms. Parallels which might clarify the needed movement to liberation may be drawn from the women's movement or black power, where women and blacks gradually articulated new meanings and worked to change existing social structures. Educators who are not themselves older adults cannot authoritatively define authentic meanings for old age. This is a collective task for older adults themselves. The educator's role is an enabler or facilitator. For this, specific skills and understandings are needed.

It may also suggest that the educational process in the theological institution may differ depending on whether the goal is the ministry of pastoral care or the ministry of education. Typically pastors-in-training need to learn by doing, to face without undue fear the realities of nursing homes and total care facilities. In that encounter they need to learn to love the vulnerable old and relate to them as they are, on their terms, and in that encounter to be able to speak (and hear) the word of truth. There is simply no other way to do this than by actually acting pastorally within a real-life situation.

It is not so clear where is the best place to begin when the task is educational and facilitative. It may well be that extensive time in a classroom setting is required to develop an understanding of the cultural, social and religious context within which perspectives on old age have developed. Then the encounter with those who are old can be true facilitation of knowledge without coercion from either party or from the dominant culture.

In the end, the account which the educator develops of the life of the old must be negotiated with those who are, in fact, old. But even here there is reason for care; not every group of older adults will be amenable to developing a deeper understanding of who they are individually and collectively within a broader social context. In most groups, it will take time and care to facilitate interest in such issues, and the educator-in-training might well be best introduced to educational ministry with older adults in a setting where such a transformative educational process is already happening.[7] The principal criteria for the choice of a setting in which to introduce the educator-in-training to older adults are: (1) whether or not a particular setting will help the educator to see beyond the mediocre and conventional image of the older adult perpetrated by mass American culture, and (2) whether or not in this situation the educator's imagination will likely be fired with excitement about the possibility of learning together for growth, for authentic self-transcendence, and even heroism in the life of the older adult.

CONCLUSION

The Center on Aging at the Presbyterian School of Christian Education has been directed by two people. Both share a concern for people in daily life who can be approached through the Church, people who grow old in a culture which doesn't much care or understand — or understands very well and doesn't want any part of it. Above all, both share a conviction that religious education can make a profound difference in the lives of older adults. However, there are emphases proper to each. The first Director, the parish pastor who trained later in life as an adult educator and gerontologist, brought to the Center his urgent sense that the Churches needed practical, immediate help if they were to be enabled to develop a full ministry with older adults. The second Director, the educator whose professional life has been concerned with how people develop religiously within their own culture, brought to the Center a vision that the Churches need imaginative and skilled facilitators who can understand and interpret the world of older adults and engage in change. These may come from differences in background and personal style. If both persons were gardeners, the first might plant vegetables and fruit to feed hungry people. The second might terrace and irrigate and get the soil right so that whatever was to grow could grow well.

Both have a strong sense of standing side-by-side, though. Religious education requires attention to landscape and inscape, to the shape of the world and to images of aging, to models of ministry and visions of wholeness. The ministry of the Church is not complete unless it includes a comprehensive educational ministry with older adults.

NOTES

1. Within a Jewish context, it is the Rabbi who is charged with religious instruction. References to "Church" in this essay are not intended to exclude religious faiths other than Christian.

2. This suggestion appears only in the 5th and final draft (October 3, 1975) of a proposal for funding to the Lily Endowment under Program V: Religious formation. It reads in part: "This proposal maintains that for the personal religious formation and spiritual well-being of theological students and faculty, a theological community should provide regular opportunities for intergenerational learning and sharing. The aged of our society . . . should contribute to and benefit from its worship, its theological discussion, and its pursuit of truth. By eating together in the dining room, by sharing classes together, and by playing and praying together, a spiritual wholeness of community can be provided that will offset the experimental isolation and age segmentation of this academic setting."

3. Albert Dimmock, Unpublished papers.

4. Henry Simmons, "Toward an Understanding of Religious Needs in Aging Persons." *The Journal of Pastoral Care*, Vol. XXXI, No. 4 (Dec. 1977), pp. 273-278.

5. Union Theological Seminary in Virginia, the School of Theology of Virginia Union University, and the Presbyterian School of Christian Education.

6. Josephine Newbury, Unpublished manuscript, 1975.

7. For an example, see S. Perlstein (1984), "A Stage for Memory: Living History Plays by Older Adults." In M. Kaminsky, (ed.) *The Uses of Reminiscence* (New York: Haworth Press), 1984, pp. 37-51.

Saint Paul School of Theology: Aging Studies

David B. Oliver, PhD

SUMMARY. Saint Paul School of Theology has an endowed program in aging studies. Aging materials have been integrated into the curriculum of both the M.Div. and D.Min. degrees. The program is headed by a tenured and trained gerontologist.

In the fall of 1979, Saint Paul School of Theology began to integrate gerontology into its seminary curriculum. Made possible through a generous gift, this United Methodist institution established both a Chair and a Center for Health and Welfare Studies with an emphasis in aging studies. Within two years the school was offering a specialization in gerontology at both the Master of Divinity and Doctor of Ministry levels, and more significantly, was integrating aging-related courses and modules into all three years of study. No student can graduate from the seminary without having experienced considerable exposure to and study of religion and aging.

THE SEMINARY

Saint Paul School of Theology is located in Kansas City, Missouri. Its primary role is to prepare persons for the ministry and mission of the Church in the world. One of thirteen United Methodist graduate theological schools, it currently offers a Master of Divinity and a Doctor of Ministry degree with approximately 150 stu-

David B. Oliver is Oubri A. Poppele Professor of Gerontology and Director of the Center of Health and Welfare Studies, Saint Paul School of Theology, Kansas City, MO.

dents enrolled in each program. In addition to the gerontology specializations, students can focus their studies in other areas (such as religious education, parish development, ethics and social change, pastoral care and counseling, etc.). Most Master of Divinity students complete their studies in three years, and are expected, before graduation, to be able to translate their personal theological stance, on the one hand, with their practice of ministry, on the other. The emphasis is on praxis. This approach to graduate theological education, the connecting of theory and practice, has played a significant role in the smooth integration of religious gerontology into the seminary curriculum.

THE HISTORY

When Miss Oubri A. Poppele decided to provide the endowment which eventually brought aging studies to the Saint Paul campus, she was a resident in a Pontiac, Illinois nursing home. Prior to her death, she left in her will a generous gift to the United Methodist Church to establish a Chair and a program in health and welfare studies at one of the thirteen church-related seminaries. Given the disproportionate number of older persons in the Church, special problems and issues related to aging, and the lack of training in gerontology at the graduate professional level, the General Board of Global Ministries of the United Methodist Church awarded the endowment to Saint Paul.

The fact that Kansas City is situated in the Midwest surrounded by four states with high percentages of older persons was also a factor in its selection. Further, the support of the original and now internationally based Shepherd's Center, the presence of the Midwest Council for Social Research in Aging, and work in aging studies at the University of Missouri Kansas City, were all factors in bringing religious gerontology to the heartland of America.

RELATION TO OTHER SEMINARIES
AND GERONTOLOGY CENTERS

The first, and current occupant of the Oubri A. Poppele Chair in Gerontology, and Director of the Center for Health and Welfare

Studies, is David B. Oliver. He came to Saint Paul from Trinity University where he served as Chairperson of the Department of Sociology and established training, research, and a degree program in gerontology. At St. Paul he has continued his professional involvement in gerontology and increased relationships with graduate theological seminaries. In the last several years, he has worked to bring "religion and aging" as a special concern and focus of study within the Association for Gerontology in Higher Education.

As an institutional representative to the Board of Directors of the National Interfaith Coalition on Aging, Oliver works with religious leaders around the country on a wide range of issues. He has introduced work in long term health care with religious homes for the aged and nursing homes. This kind of academic and community involvement is essential if a seminary-based program in aging studies is to be effective, up-to-date, and constantly growing with the field. This is particularly the case for such a new brand of specialization as "religious gerontology."

Saint Paul School of Theology has been directly and indirectly involved in a number of local, regional, and national conferences, workshops, symposia, seminars, etc., connecting religion and aging. This includes a number of different universities and colleges, denominations, health care institutions, and seminaries. Again, given the highly specialized nature of religious gerontology, professionals in it are often isolated in their respective settings. Cooperative programming, training, research, and development needs to be coordinated through some kind of organizational network of professional relationships.

DEVELOPING CONTENT AND ALTERNATIVE EDUCATIONAL STRATEGIES

A variety of approaches and strategies designed to prepare clergy and other professional leaders to work with older persons are possible. The style and method with which gerontology becomes integrated into religious education is not as important, however, as the nature of its content. What will make aging studies different in the religious context will be the added dimension of how one's theology, on the one hand, will influence one's practice of ministry, on the other. For clergy and other religious educators, it is not enough to know some of the critical variables affecting the physiological, psychological, social, and emotional worlds of older persons. While a social and behavioral science approach to aging is necessary, it is not sufficient. There is more to it. Any strategy within the context of religious education must view theology and ministry as having a praxis connection. To omit this relationship will reduce one's educational program to the level of that being offered in secular schools.

Theological and religious gerontology needs to be holistic in nature. That is, the physical, mental, social, and spiritual dimensions of aging must all be included. The sciences (social and natural) are very important in this regard. The wealth of information which has been assembled over the last three decades is essential to any aging program. The key is how to integrate this information into the context of theological understanding and, at the same time, into the practice of ministry. While a number of strategies have been tried, and many more are to be developed, the suggestions below offer a sampling of alternatives.

Aging and Religion Training Modules

One way to introduce aging-related content into seminary education is to integrate it into courses already established in the curriculum. At Saint Paul School of Theology, for example, gerontology has become part of a required second year core unit which focuses, among other things, on pastoral care and religious education. Students are exposed to the world of the nursing home, and they study and reflect on ministry in this setting. This, in turn, raises issues about aging, generally, and how the church/synagogue/parish is responding to the multiple needs of the "well elderly" as well as the "frail elderly." Since this particular core unit is team taught (by a theologian and a person with training and experience in an applied field), theology and ministry are brought together. A special advantage of this strategy is that since the gerontological input is integrated into a required core unit, all students are exposed and must respond to it.

Given overloaded curricula in most seminaries, it is often much simpler to incorporate these kinds of modules into existing courses. Moreover, by introducing gerontological concerns in biblical studies, historical studies, preaching, worship, "missional" and other areas, students receive not only a comprehensive exposure, they are able to see more clearly the connection of it all to their ministry.

At Saint Paul, the person responsible for integrating aging-related content into core units works closely with the mentors who have the main responsibility for the class. This is a critical piece of the process. The aging material must make sense within the context of overall course goals and objectives. If a different set of mentors is assigned for the following year, a new and different syllabus may have to be prepared. As a result, the aging-related content may change as well. In some cases the gerontological information is spread out over the course of the term, while in others, it appears as a special unit presented on consecutive days. A latent function of this kind of scheduling is the interaction and sharing which occurs between the "gerontology" professor(s) and the "theology" professor(s). The aging part never stands alone.

Short Courses, Classes, or Seminars

Short courses, which meet once per week for a couple of hours, will fit into most curriculum structures. These courses can be more specialized (e.g., "Ethnicity, Aging, and the Church"; "Hospice Training"; "Aging and Ministry in the Rural Midwest"; "Developing Lay Ministries With Older Adults"; "Preaching, Worship, and Older Persons"; "Biblical Perspectives on Aging"; and more), and can provide an opportunity for a greater variety of faculty participation. These courses can be made available for continuing education students as well as for full-time seminary students. At Saint Paul there is the added advantage of offering each year, a required seminar on "Ageism" to all first year students. This fits well with similar required seminars in the areas of "Racism," "Sexism," and "Classism."

Short courses, continuing education classes, and seminars also allow the institution to bring in adjunct or visiting faculty. This expands the ability of the seminary to meet the needs of those in the local church as well as the needs of full-time students. Moreover, if ecumenical and interreligious in nature, this approach can be cost-effective as a result of the numbers it can attract. Coordination, content, and promotion are critical variables to success.

At Saint Paul there is an attempt to involve the regular full-time faculty in the aging-related short courses, continuing education offerings, and seminars. That is, while gerontology is integrated into the regular curriculum in the manner described above, theology is integrated into the more specialized aging short courses in much the same way. This not only assures the continuing connection between theory and practice, it continues to nurture the authenticity of religion and aging as an integral part of seminary concerns.

Electives, Specializations, and Certificate Programs

A series of classes which can be taken independently or with the intent of completing a specialization or certification in religious gerontology is, of course, more ambitious. This has been accomplished at Saint Paul at both the Master of Divinity and Doctor of Ministry levels. Courses on "The Processes of Aging," "Communication With Older Persons," "Death and Dying," and "The World of Nursing Homes" are included. The need here is to have a faculty member, an adjunct faculty member, a part-time faculty member, or a gerontological consultant to provide the needed coordination and development of such an undertaking.

Developing this kind of program requires resources and commitments from many segments of the seminary system. It needs to be a cooperative venture. The resources of the Poppele endowment, administrative support, and faculty involvement clearly makes this possible at Saint Paul School of Theology. In other settings, if faculty support is not clearly evident, it is important that gerontological studies not become isolated from the rest of the curriculum. If the focus on aging becomes a free-standing enterprise, it will only survive as long as the person who teaches it is employed. Some seminaries have experienced the loss of gerontology in their curricula simply because the person who taught it retired. A commitment to its inclusion needs to be made from the Board of Trustees.

At Saint Paul, the specialization in gerontology at the Master of Divinity level includes the following:

1. Twelve hours of coursework to be selected in consultation with a faculty advisor from among the following: RE 310 Faith Development in Life Stages; RE 311 Teaching/Learning: Life-Long Process; RE 216 Ministry With Adults; HW 355 Processes of Aging (required of all students); HW 365 Aging and Ministry in the Rural Midwest; HW 368 Hospice Training; HW 370 Communication With Older Adults; HW 375 The World of Nursing Homes; HW 380 The Church's Ministry With Older Persons; HW 385 Racial and Ethnic Minorities: Aging-Related Issues; PC 422 Seminar: Ethical Issues in Modern Bio-Medicine; HW 500 Directed Study; HW 520 Supervised Field Work (required unless waived); HW 590 Research.

2. Four hours of Supervised Field Work (HW 520). Arranged and supervised by the Director of the Center of Health and Welfare studies. These hours should be scheduled following the completion of the required Processes of Aging (HW 355) course. The supervised field work required may be waived if demonstration of proficiency in ministry with older adults is provided by the student.

3. A professional paper (essay) in the student's area of interest; guidelines are provided. Evaluation of this work is incorporated in a concluding conference with the Director of the Health and Welfare Center and one other faculty member to assess the student's professional readiness for ministry with older persons.

The specialization in gerontology at the Doctor of Ministry level is, with the exception of a three week Exploratory Phase and selected seminars, an off-campus program of study. It is an advanced professional degree designed for those who desire an academic program which deepens and broadens their practice of ministry in the area of aging. It requires a Master of Divinity (or its equivalent) as a prerequisite.

The D.Min. program incorporates a method of personalized learning which both challenges and supports the student in the reaffirmation of the Gospel; it strengthens areas of weakness; and it blends the unique skills of the student into a holistic, focused ministry. Following the Exploratory Phase, which has as its concentration the rethinking of one's theological center and practice of ministry, is the Praxis Credo Phase. Here the student brings together his or her theology, aging, and the practice of ministry into a single statement (30-50 page credo) which is presented for evaluation at a faculty conference. The final phase, the Field Project Phase, allows the student the opportunity to test and/or implement a proposed model of ministry (a written research document) which is based on and derived from his or her praxis credo. This, too, is followed by a faculty evaluation conference.

Field Work Opportunities and Experience

Praxis is achieved when a particular perspective is implemented or when a particular perspective grows out of the experience itself. Opportunities for students (full-time and continuing education) to encounter the world directly and then to reflect on the meaning of that experience within the context of their theological stance is an excellent teaching/learning methodology. Well coordinated settings — such as in churches, synagogues, parishes, retirement communities, nursing homes, social service agencies, senior centers, area agencies on aging, etc. — lead to valuable relationships with professionals and para-professionals outside the seminary who then become parts of the larger gerontological training program.

One concern in the field of religion and aging, not always encountered in other areas, is the extent to which stipends are available. For nearly every one hundred potential field work opportunities in aging, fewer than ten will be able to pay a reasonable stipend.

At Saint Paul School of Theology, if a student is pursuing a specialization in gerontology (at either the Master of Divinity or Doctor of Ministry level), he or she is required, in part, to work and study "in the field." While stipends are available in some community settings, there will be cases in which the work must be done on a volunteer basis. It is gratifying to note, however, that nearly all of the churches in which a student is learning to connect his or her theology and practical ministry, a stipend is provided.

Lay Training

Lay empowering should be the goal of most pastors, rabbis, and priests. The theological academy is especially equipped to provide this kind of training. As stated earlier, the most successful and creative ministries with older adults are usually developed and nurtured by lay persons.

It has been the experience at Saint Paul that when the training of laity is taken from the classroom into the midst of where older adults confront the world, the results are enhanced. This is particularly the case in ministries involving older adults. Lay persons (regardless of their age) are often isolated from what is going on in our society regarding the older population. Knowledge of the availability and accessibility of resources is often limited. Lay training "in the field" meets this need.

Finally, any methodology connecting religion and aging should draw heavily on the experiences and wisdom of older persons themselves. Lay training should not be confined to the classroom nor isolated from older persons any more than training offered to regular, full-time graduate theological students.

Continuing Gerontological Education for Clergy and Others

Since the Oubri A. Poppele Center was established on the Saint Paul campus, a number and variety of continuing education opportunities have been developed and sponsored. These have included: pre-retirement seminars for clergy and laity, seminars for church women's organizations, special workshops for chaplains, clergy and staff working in institutional settings, consultations for the leadership of several denominational groups, and special training for professionals and para-professionals who work in social service and governmental agencies which supervise and provide services for the elderly. Attendance at these educational events has ranged from twenty to two hundred persons.

A consistent finding over the last eight years is the extent of participation on the part of clergy and laity. The former group is less likely to attend continuing education events (connecting religion and aging) in large numbers unless their denominational leadership formally encourages it. Laity, on the other hand, tend to be eager participants. Since the most successful programs of ministry with older persons are generally developed and managed by lay persons, perhaps this differential response to continuing education in gerontology should not be a concern. Yet, it may represent some deeper, more challenging, issues. The Poppele Center is currently involved in a major research project in the state of Kansas which will address this and other concerns.

It has been fruitful to hold a number of events beyond the Saint Paul campus. This has included the sponsorship of regional conferences and seminars in other states. More specifically, it has been easier to take the training to those who want it, than insist that they come to Kansas City to get it. Local churches have been very cooperative in planning, developing, advertising, and hosting continuing education events with Saint Paul. Various United Methodist Conferences and Districts and other denominational groups have put together cooperative programs.

Training Faculty in Graduate Theological Education

The early growth of gerontology in colleges and universities was made possible, in large part, by interuniversity training programs funded by the federal government. Post- and pre-doctoral fellowships in gerontology were made available to persons pursuing degrees in a variety of disciplines. Leading gerontologists in the United States became mentors at training seminars located at a number of different sites. The outcome was the establishment of courses, certification tracks, and degree programs in higher education from Maine to California. Ph.D. degree granting institutions and two-year (post-high school) associate degree schools, and everything in between, became involved. At the same time, national associations were formed and expanded, and a body of research and knowledge began to accumulate at an exponential rate.

The same kind of training plan is needed in graduate theological education. There are faculty members who have an interest in religion and aging-related issues, but who have not had the opportunity to study in this area. Needed are interseminary training programs involving not only a variety of denominational and faith stances but, also, the coming together of religious educators most interested in advancing our knowledge of how theology and aging connect. Symposia and dialogue, cooperative research projects, and collaboration are needed. Although a particular denomination or faith may find it easier to work within its own ranks, the growth of religious gerontology will be more enhanced by ecumenical and interreligious sharing. At this level there are sufficient resources in personnel to provide the kind of leadership required for the needed training and development. What is more problematic, however, are the financial resources required to organize and implement such a strategy.

At the national level, only a handful of religious groups have made a substantial commitment to aging-related concerns. Many have made rhetorical statements and taken philosophical positions, but what is often suggested and encouraged, lacks the kind of power and authority required for a follow-through program of action. Perhaps a grass-roots movement will demand that something more be done. Perhaps a progressive religious leader with a bit of charisma will set the standard. This part of the story has yet to be written.

What is certain is the ubiquitous presence of older persons within the church/synagogue/parish. Religious bodies cannot continue to idolize youth at the expense of elderly members. Their very survival may depend on how well they respond to the latter third of the life cycle rather than how well they do at the beginning of it.

At Saint Paul School of Theology a major effort has been made to involve as many of the faculty as possible in the ongoing gerontological enterprise. The team teaching approach to graduate theological education has clearly helped in this regard. However, in addition to involving faculty in teaching, the Oubri A. Poppele Center began publishing the *Quarterly Papers on Religion and Aging*. Now in its fourth year, this internationally subscribed to publication has attracted not only faculty and other professional contributors from outside the seminary, it has included contributors from within as well. Four Saint Paul faculty members have already had one or more articles published. In a recent book, *New Directions in Religion and Aging* (The Haworth Press, 1987; edited by David Oliver), the same number of faculty from Saint Paul School of Theology joined ten others in contributing chapters. This kind of intellectual activity and sharing helps to integrate gerontology into the overall seminary curriculum.

And finally, faculty trips to professional meetings in gerontology (e.g., the Gerontological Society of America, the Association for Gerontology in Higher Education, the American Society on Aging, the National Interfaith Coalition on Aging, etc.) are encouraged and supported. This is also the case for students specializing in gerontology.

SAINT PAUL GRADUATES
IN RELIGIOUS GERONTOLOGY

As stated earlier, all students at the seminary receive training in aging studies. In fact, it is impossible to graduate from Saint Paul School of Theology without having been exposed to religious gerontology. This occurs in the first and second year of the curriculum. Students desiring further work, and possibly a specialization in gerontology, can enroll in a wide range of electives during their third and final year of study.

The first Doctor of Ministry specialization in aging was awarded in 1984. Since that time, nine have graduated, and sixteen are currently in the program. They represent fifteen different states and the District of Columbia. The first Master of Divinity student specializing in gerontology graduated the same year. Thirteen have completed the specialization since that time, six will graduate this May, and a new group of six will focus on aging during their third year of study in 1988-89. Thus twenty-five D.Min. and twenty-five M.Div. students will have completed or will be completing their specializations by the end of the next academic year.

RESEARCH CONNECTING
RELIGION AND AGING

Earl Brewer, of Emory University and Candler School of Theology, has made the best case, albeit pessimistic, for more research in the field of religion and aging.[1] The Gerontology emphasis at Saint Paul has not included, to any significant degree, the kind of excellent research projects which he proposes. This year, however, marks the first major research effort to date.

An extensive questionnaire is being mailed, with the support of the Bishop, to every United Methodist Church in the State of Kansas. It will determine the nature and extent of ministries with older persons, and examine differences by size of church, age composition, location of church, size of staff, and more. It will also explore problems that clergy encounter in their ministry with older adults, and will look at the extent of cooperation that exists with other churches as well as with community programs and agencies. The survey was designed in such a way that it can be replicated in other states. The information collected will be useful not only in terms of program development and planning, but will also be valuable to local congregations who will be supplied with the results so that they can further empower older adults in their continuing service to the church and community.

COMMUNITY INVOLVEMENT

Central to preparing students for professional ministry with older adults is the need to involve them in a wide range of community programs and activities. Saint Paul is therefore continually seeking persons and agencies with whom a mutually beneficial working relationship can be established. This has been the case with area nursing homes, Shepherd's Centers, Area Agencies on Aging, hospitals, bio-ethics centers, local colleges and universities, retirement communities, housing projects, emergency shelters, and a number of organizations that provide direct services to older persons. Students utilize these settings in meeting class requirements, in directed research projects, and in making one of them their "student setting" for ministry. This connection between the seminary and the community is essential to theological education.

Prognosis for the Future

The scope of gerontology has indeed captured the imagination of persons from a variety of fields and disciplines, but it is only recently that it has begun to impact theologians and those who minister on a daily basis with persons who are now in the last third of life. While professional training in aging in graduate theological seminaries has been initiated, it is somewhat perplexing that religion is again one of the last social institutions to deal with a subject so central to its mission and purpose. Older persons are not only disproportionately represented among the various denominations and religious faiths in the United States, they are often both recipients and providers of care for other older persons in their communities. The potential use for gerontological knowledge with and among this vast collection of individuals is unlimited. Leadership and direction are desired and needed.[2]

During the past three years, movement has clearly begun in a number of centers around the country. Professional societies in the *secular* world are increasingly adding "religion" as a significant variable in aging studies, and professional groups in the *sacred* world are adding "aging" as a significant variable in their religious studies. The prognosis is good. There is a place for religious gerontology in graduate theological education. Saint Paul School of Theology has not looked back since the inception of its program in 1979. The future lies ahead, not behind.

NOTES

    1. Earl Brewer "Research in Religion and Aging: An Unlikely Scenario," In David B. Oliver (Ed.), *New Directions in Religion and Aging*. (New York: The Haworth Press), 1987, pp. 91-102.
    2. David B. Oliver "Gerontology in a Graduate Theological Seminary," *Journal of Religion & Aging*, Vol. 1, No. 1. (Fall, 1984), pp. 87-101.

Southwestern Baptist Theological Seminary and Baylor University: Ministerial Gerontological Education

Ben E. Dickerson, PhD
Dennis R. Myers, PhD
Lucian E. Coleman, Jr., EdD
Derrel R. Watkins, EdD

SUMMARY. A sensitive account of the efforts of a seminary and a university to develop joint programs in gerontology with emphasis on religion, ministry and aging. Leaders interested in or involved in such arrangements will benefit by this case study.

There is an urgent need to equip more effectively the seminarian with gerontological education. This urgency comes from the increasing number of congregational members that fall in the age category of 55 years or older. Likewise, the increased need of the younger congregational member to respond appropriately to older family members and friends within their religious institution heightens the need for effective programmatic responses within churches and synagogues. Furthermore, seminaries are not providing an adequate curriculum response in the preparation of religious leaders who can address the issues resulting from an aged society. Therefore, the purpose of this paper is to demonstrate how a private university and a theological seminary responded to the challenge of gerontological education for ministers. To accomplish this purpose,

---

Ben E. Dickerson is Professor of Sociology and Gerontology and Dennis R. Myers is Assistant Professor of Social Work and Gerontology, both at Baylor University Institute of Gerontological Studies. Lucian E. Coleman, Jr. is Professor of Adult Education and Derrel R. Watkins is Professor of Social Work, both at Southwestern Baptist Theological Seminary.

the authors will address three objectives: (1) describe the development and progress of each institution's individual and collective effort in producing graduates with a more comprehensive knowledge of the elderly; (2) discuss the key factors which contribute to a successful educational venture by a university and seminary; and (3) identify issues which need to be resolved to insure continuation of the joint enterprise between two educational institutions.

The authors will introduce the reader to each educational institution's approach to gerontological education and then highlight the sequence of events which led to a formal memorandum of understanding between the two. Additionally, key factors responsible for the effectiveness of the linkage of the University and Seminary will be discussed. Issues created by the conjoint effort will be discussed to include how they were or were not resolved. The authors conclude by giving a brief summary and a statement of implications which this case study might have for other higher education institutions wishing to pursue such a reciprocal relationship.

GERONTOLOGY AT BAYLOR UNIVERSITY

Baylor University is investing in the developing of the Institute of Gerontological Studies designed to broaden understanding of the life experiences and to respond to the needs of older persons. In this section, a brief history of the development of gerontological study at Baylor University will precede a description of the current instruction, research and service offerings of the Institute. A presentation of future directions for gerontology at this University will follow the discussion.

The increasing number of older persons in the nation as a whole and within Southern Baptist congregations sparked an initiative which led to the formal introduction of gerontology at Baylor University. This initiative came from the President of the University, the Director of Denominational Relations, and faculty members within the Department of Sociology. These individuals recognized that very little was being done in Southern Baptist institutions to prepare professionals for intervention with the rapidly increasing number of older persons in churches. Representatives of Baylor University contacted the University of North Texas (formerly North

Texas State University), which had the most well-established gerontological graduate program in the Southwest. In 1976, a graduate degree program consisting of approximately 36 hours was established. The program was designed to be multidisciplinary with both external and internal advisement committees available to assist in the development of a curriculum which would be responsive to the needs of students. To complement the graduate degree, a certificate program was also established for persons who desired gerontological education but who chose not to pursue a formal degree. From the beginning, it was clear that this program should prepare students to enable persons in their independence, their dignity, and their involvement in life. The objective was to reduce or possibly eliminate the necessity of institutionalization. As the program grew, the emphasis on the multidisciplinary nature of graduate education also increased. It became evident that gerontology should have its own budget and be structured as a separate and distinct entity from the Department of Sociology, in which the Institute was housed initially. In 1981, university administration approved a proposal which created the Institute of Gerontological Studies.

The objective of the newly created Institute is to provide instruction, research, and service which focuses on the needs of persons aged 65 years of age and older. The curriculum of the Institute's graduate program is designed to prepare students for professional involvement with older persons and organizations concerned with their well-being. The degree programs are administered under the auspices of a multidisciplinary committee which includes representation from such academic specializations as biology, business, communications, computer science, educational psychology, health and physical education, home economics, music, oral history, psychology, religion, social work, and sociology. The Institute offers degree programs designed to meet the needs of students having a variety of career objectives within the broad field of gerontology. The first degree program leads to a Master of Science in Gerontology, which requires 43 hours of instruction and research, including a six-hour internship or thesis. One of the special emphasis areas within the Master of Science degree is that of religion and aging. Within this emphasis, graduate students are prepared for a specialty in ministry with older persons within the church setting. Tuition support for students pursuing this special emphasis is provided by benefactors who recognize the importance of gerontology to religious organizations. As the curriculum for the Master of Science degree developed, it became evident that the certificate program would need to be eliminated. The reason for this action was that there were other programs in the state that were offering various levels of certification and it was very difficult for students to be respected for their academic achievement when another person with only six hours could also say they had a gerontological certification. Because of this dilution of the meaning of the certificate program, it was eliminated as an academic option for the graduate student. In 1986, a new degree program, the Master of Clinical Gerontology, was included in the Institute's graduate offerings. This degree program provides an opportunity for advanced study in gerontology for baccalaureate-prepared health professionals and is designed to help health professionals increase their knowledge and skills to work more effectively with the elderly.

Student interest in gerontological education at Baylor University has grown. Since the inception of the instructional program, approximately sixty students have graduated. These graduates have been successful in finding employment within human service organizations concerned with older persons. A number continued their education at a theological seminary and some have been interested in obtaining a doctorate so that they can teach at the seminary or university level. Graduates are also employed as ministers to senior adults within local churches or have located positions within religious organizations on the state or national level.

The Institute's curricular response to gerontology is augmented by a web of extramural relationships with organizations interested in the spiritual aspects of aging. Organizations which have been particularly supportive of the development of curriculum include the Association of Gerontology in Higher Education (AGHE); National Council on Aging (NCOA); and National Interfaith Coalition on Aging (NICA). Organizations such as the Texas A&M College of Medicine, the Baylor College of Dentistry, public and private medical centers within the region, and three Veterans Administration medical facilities support the Health emphasis, which is particularly strong in the Institute's curriculum. These interorganizational relationships are the vehicle for the effective internship program established within the Institute. In the case of students pursuing the religion and aging emphasis, faculty of the Institute work very closely with church and/or denominational agencies to insure that the student is provided with an opportunity to translate gerontological knowledge into the ministry setting.

To complement the religion and aging emphasis within the graduate curriculum, faculty of the Institute are involved in research programs which will better inform ministry efforts with older persons. Currently, investigations are being conducted in the area of family relationships in later life with particular focus on sibling solidarity. Other research efforts include investigations into the life experiences of older probationers as well as incarcerated older females. Students are encouraged to become actively involved in these programs and consider the implications of research for their ministry.

In addition to the Institute's involvement in graduate education and research, the Institute is involved in activities which directly impact the intellectual and spiritual lives of older persons. For example, the Institute sponsors noncredit educational offerings, such as the Herbert H. Reynolds Summer School for Retired Persons, the National Foster Grandparent Jamboree, and an Elderhostel offering. The faculty of the Institute provide consultation and workshop experiences for professional and lay leaders of religious organizations interested in the spiritual well-being of older persons.

As is reflected in the historical and contemporary review of gerontology at Baylor University, there has been an emphasis on the spiritual aspects of aging. It is projected that innovations in the area of curriculum, research, and service will strengthen this emphasis. One of the planning objectives for the Institute is to increase linkages with a wide range of religious organizations concerned with spirituality and aging. It is believed that a stronger interfaith emphasis will contribute significantly to the preparation of students for ministry with adults as well as promote the possibility of research and continuing education programs which cut across theological and denominational boundaries. Faculty of the Institute are particularly interested in giving emphasis to the older woman. They have found that religious organizations often limit ministry to the widow and thereby ignore other salient issues faced by women in later life, such as poverty, health promotion, spiritual development, and the requirements related to being a care giver, older parent, and grandparent.

In the future, the faculty of the Institute will be involved in developing policies and programs which focus on linking generations so that each can utilize the unique resources of the other. In doing this, heavy reliance will be placed on oral history as an important mechanism in strengthening intergenerational relations within religious organizations. To complement the emphasis on intergenerational relations, programs with the Baylor University School of Music are planned so that students will have a better understanding of the role that religious music plays in the spiritual development of the older person. The demographic realities of aging within the international community produces a need for educational services to clergy and lay persons concerned with spiritual issues in later life in other countries. One implication of this trend is that missionaries and their families will require assistance with retirement and other issues which accompany old age. The faculty of the Institute will provide specialized educational programs which prepare persons who have a desire to address the spiritual needs of the elderly in their own country. Often, international students are not eligible to enroll in regular graduate study and require specialized programs to equip them to meet their objectives. Under the special foreign student program developed within the Institute, individuals can pursue their educational goals in gerontology without having to be accepted in the graduate school. Long-range plans developed for the Institute include four world regional conferences over a ten-year period which would be a joint effort with the Southern Baptist Convention Foreign Mission Board. The purpose of these international conferences would be to prepare missionaries to be more responsive to the needs of older persons within the designated country.

Effectiveness in ministry with adults will be related to the extent to which the religious organization minimizes chronological age and emphasizes intergenerational relationships. In the past, students in the Institute have been involved in programs which demonstrate that ethnicity in later life is a resource rather than a problem. For example, graduate students work closely with a Jewish congregation in the local area to establish a day program for the older Jewish person. The "Chevarah" program was developed because the publicly funded senior centers did not respond to the needs of the older Jewish person.

Future expansion in linkages between the Institute and ethnic groups is expected. The dissemination of knowledge and pragmatic innovations to practitioners within religious organizations will be a special focus of the faculty. The hiatus between available knowledge and practice will be bridged through increased continuing education offerings as well as a clearing-house which will be available to local ministers and denominational officials. In sum, meeting the spiritual needs of older persons will be a priority in program design and resource allocation into the twenty-first century.

GERONTOLOGY AT SOUTHWESTERN BAPTIST THEOLOGICAL SEMINARY

Southwestern Baptist Theological Seminary was chartered in 1908 for the purpose of providing theological education for men and women preparing for Christian ministry. Active concern for the older members of church and society permeates the life of the Seminary in a variety of ways. Course work focusing on older adulthood is supplemented by continuing education conferences, an annual endowed lectureship, a campus organization devoted to ministry with the aging, and a substantial collection of resources for the study of gerontology in the Seminary's library system.

Southwestern Seminary has offered course work related to older adulthood over the past thirty years. In 1915 the department of religious education was created and served as the primary focal point for gerontological education within the Seminary. For example, course content related to older adults was included in the educational administration courses as early as the 1950s. In 1955, a course entitled Religious Education in Later Adulthood marked the first course offering dedicated to the study of later life. In the early 1960s, ethics courses in the School of Theology began to reflect an interest in aging. By 1970, a course entitled Pastoral Care of the Aging was one indicator of the Seminary's growing commitment to gerontological education. During this period the Seminary established a cooperative relationship with the University of North Texas (formerly North Texas State University) which allowed cross-sharing of faculty in course offerings. A member of the Southwestern faculty participated in the development of the National Interfaith Coalition on Aging (NICA) and conducted seminal research on seminary preparation for ministry with the elderly. The faculty member also represented the Southern Baptist Convention on the board of NICA. In cooperation with the Southern Baptist Convention's Sunday School Board, Southwestern Seminary hosted the first national conference on religion and aging for Southern Baptists. All of the above mentioned course offerings and activities point to the longstanding commitment of Southwestern Seminary to preparation of students for ministry with older adults. This rich heritage of involvement and interest served as a very adequate foundation for the development of seminary study in gerontology in the 1980s.

The current emphasis on aging at Southwestern is motivated by a conviction expressed by the psalmist: "The righteous shall flourish like a palm tree . . . they will still bear fruit in old age" (Psalms 92:12,14). Seminary training should equip ministers to promote spiritual well-being through every stage of life. Faculty at the Seminary are also convinced that the demand for ministers with specialized training in gerontology will continue to grow. Currently, the Seminary does not offer a degree in gerontology. One reason for this is the distinctive mission of a theological institution. Since a central purpose is to provide a theological education, all degree programs at the Seminary rest upon a foundation of Biblical/theological studies, in addition to offering technical training in specialized areas of ministry. It is not the purpose of the seminary to duplicate degree offerings in gerontology that are available within college and university settings. Therefore, faculty advise those who do not wish to function as vocational Christian ministers in churches or staff-related denominational settings to consider the possibility of study in a university-based gerontology program.

Seminary students may elect to pursue a concentration in gerontology in two master's level degree programs: the Master of Arts in Religious Education (M.A.R.E.) and the Master of Arts in Church Social Services (M.A.C.S.S.). Those who are preparing for church-related educational ministries but who wish to give special emphasis to ministries with older persons usually select the M.A.R.E. program with a concentration in gerontology. Others who wish to engage in specialized social ministries with older persons in church and/or denominational agencies are advised to pursue the M.A.C.S.S. degree with a concentration in gerontology. Each degree program consists of a core of required courses in theology, religious education, and other professional studies, in addition to a sequence of courses in the student's chosen concentration. The pastor continues to play a key role in ministry to senior adults in the church and denomination. While the Seminary does not offer a pastoral degree program specifically focused in gerontology, M.Div. students are encouraged to select elective courses from the gerontology offerings provided. In addition to these courses, the Seminary periodically offers doctor of ministry seminars and colloquia in the field of gerontology.

In 1986, the Kirk-Gulledge Christian Gerontology Endowment Fund was established to support the infusion of gerontological knowledge within the Seminary and the denomination. On an annual basis, distinguished leaders in the field of religion and gerontology lecture on the Southwestern campus, and continuing education events are frequently planned in conjunction with these annual lectures. Other conferences and workshops are offered from time to time through the continuing education program at Southwestern. Another benefit of the endowment fund was the appointment of a task force to oversee the development of the gerontology program at the Seminary. Membership on this task force includes faculty and key administrators within the Seminary, directors of Southern Baptist Convention organizations, and a representative from Baylor University. As a further encouragement for gerontological education on campus, Southwestern Seminary sponsors the only existing campus chapter of the Southern Baptist Association for Ministries with the Aging (SBAMA). This campus organization carries studies in aging far beyond the class by sponsoring field trips to retirement centers and health care facilities and lectures by expert resource persons, taking student groups to attend symposia on gerontology at nearby universities, and providing opportunities for students to attend state and national meetings of the SBAMA.

In future years, it is expected that the emphasis on gerontology in the Seminary curriculum and in continuing education offerings will expand. Because of the specialized nature of theological education mentioned above, it is not anticipated that there will be a rapid increase in the number of course offerings related to gerontology. However, faculty of the Seminary are committed to the task of enhancing the ability of ministers to work with older persons through offering selective courses and, just as importantly, working with faculty members to include an emphasis on older adulthood in a wide range of courses. It is believed that integrating gerontological content into the generalist curriculum and providing opportunities for intense specialization will create the most effective method of serving the older person in the church and community. Evangelism and the older person will be a specialized area which will receive considerable emphasis in the future. The progress made in expanding the gerontology curriculum over the past three years will be continued in the future. Two new courses emphasizing creative thinking in older adulthood will be offered during the 1989-90 academic year. One course will be offered at the master's level and the other at the doctoral level. Concerning continuing education programs in gerontology, it is anticipated that conferences on aging in conjunction with the annual Kellog lectures in Christian gerontology will continue and focus on providing pastors, ministers of education, ministers with senior adults, and senior adult program administrators with helpful gerontological content. Specialized conferences and workshops for ministers, such as "Making the Most of Your Ministry in the Later Years," "Retirement as a New Career," and "Caring for the Caregivers in Your Congregation," will be offered. Training programs specifically designed for volunteer workers with senior adults in the church will also be organized.

Southwestern Baptist Theological Seminary is responding to the challenge of older persons in decisive ways: course offerings in gerontology backed up by an expanding collection of library resources; a significant endowment fund dedicated to research and instruction in aging; a multidisciplinary task force, coordinating current program offerings and forging plans for the future; and an endowed lectureship in gerontology. At the heart of this expanding effort is a growing nucleus of students, faculty members, administrators, and donors who have pooled energies and resources in the cause of gerontology at the Seminary.

THE BAYLOR AND THE SOUTHWESTERN SEMINARY RECIPROCAL RELATIONSHIP

A mutual interest in gerontological education and research as well as a sense of responsibility to the local church and the staff workers in the various state and national denominational offices served as a primary impetus for establishing a working relationship between the Institute of Gerontological Studies at Baylor University and the Southwestern Baptist Theological Seminary. Both recognized the challenge that older persons extend to religious congregations and were committed to the kind of reciprocal exchanges which would further denominational responses to older persons. The late 1970s was an informal period of much discussion and preparation for the more formalized agreements which would follow in the 1980s.

Since the inception of the Institute, faculty leadership at Baylor expressed a desire to establish a relationship with Southern Baptist seminaries in various parts of the nation. This linkage activity was related to a larger objective of establishing an aging network among Baptist colleges, institutions, and seminaries. While there was considerable interest within these institutions in cooperative relationships, there was a need for a catalyst to seek out the kinds of linkages which would benefit the member institutions as well as older persons. The faculty of the Institute determined to be that catalyst within the network. One external influence which encouraged this kind of activity was the fact that the federal government was withdrawing support for aging programs and encouraging local communities and private organizations to work more closely to address the needs of the elderly.

After considerable informal negotiating and preparation, a joint meeting of the administrators from Baylor University and Southwestern Seminary was held on April 1, 1981 in Waco, Texas. The presidents of both institutions affirmed the statement of purpose for the meeting and indicated their support for the development of a formal letter of agreement between the two institutions. Several

items discussed in the meeting reflected their willingness to participate in a joint relationship. For example, the president of Baylor
University indicated that seminarians attending Baylor for the purpose of studying aging would receive financial assistance so that
they would not be required to pay more for credit hours than at the
Seminary. It was also agreed that faculty involved in the gerontology program within each institution who desire joint appointment at
both schools would submit their credentials to the appropriate graduate school for approval. The possibilities for a cooperative internship program were discussed as were various programs in aging
which the two schools could sponsor. It was also suggested that a
Humanities in Aging conference be held annually with the location
of the meeting in Ft. Worth, Texas, one year and in Waco, Texas,
the next. As a result of this meeting, a formal letter of agreement
was signed to provide a basis of understanding between the two
institutions concerning their responsibilities in a cooperative program in gerontology. January 1, 1982 was the date for initiation of
this agreement. The objectives of this agreement are as follows:

—To develop a comprehensive approach to the study and practice of gerontology which emphasizes the wholeness of the
  individual.
—To share institutional resources related to the field of aging
  including faculty, staff and curricular structures.
—To expand academic opportunities for students interested in
  the field of aging by offering credit courses at the graduate
  level, joint degree programs, field placement and internships.
—To provide academic counseling for students who are developing theses/dissertations/projects.
—To produce, maintain and disseminate gerontological information which is available to Southern Baptist Convention consti-
  uencies and other interested religious groups.
—To enhance Southern Baptist operational efforts in the field of
  aging.
—To sponsor conferences, workshops, seminars and other programs to promote professional development and continuing
  education opportunities.

—To assist graduates in their searches for vocational placements.

To complement the objectives, it was agreed that Seminary faculty participating in the agreement would be granted Baylor adjunct faculty status and participating Baylor faculty would be granted Seminary adjunct status. Specific guidelines for handling matriculation and credit notation issues were provided in the agreement as were mechanisms for handling communication and financial arrangements for students involved with both institutions. The meeting which generated the working agreement can best be characterized as one of acceptance, excitement, and an eagerness to move forward. After the meeting, faculty at the Seminary returned with an enhanced commitment to gerontological education at their institution and a heightened interest in developing ways both the University and the Seminary could work together. As a result of faculty effort, the first educational institutional chapter of the Southern Baptist Association for Ministry with the Aged (SBAMA) was established. Students began to travel between Ft. Worth, Texas, and Waco, Texas, to attend special lectures in gerontology sponsored by both the Seminary and Baylor. This joint sponsorship resulted in the provision of financial resources which made it possible to bring nationally known leaders in the field of gerontology to both campuses.

After the signing of the letter of agreement, an exchange of faculty resources between the two institutions was initiated. Gerontology courses taught by Baylor faculty at Southwestern include: The Physiology of Aging; Aging and Mental Health; and Death and Dying. Courses taught by Seminary faculty at Baylor University include: The Church and the Older Person; and Mid-Life. Very early in the program, two or three students from the Seminary began their work at Baylor. At the conclusion of their studies at the Seminary and at Baylor, they had met the requirements to receive a Master of Arts degree in Religious Education, as well as a Master of Science in Gerontology at Baylor. As will be mentioned, when the future plans for this relationship are discussed below, it is anticipated that the development of the joint degree program which is currently pending will result in a marked increase in the number of students receiving degrees from the two institutions.

In addition to the contribution each institution has made to the gerontological content in their respective curricula, the two institutions have also been successfully involved in efforts to enrich the Southern Baptist response to their older membership. In 1983, Baylor and Southwestern Seminary jointly sponsored the National Conference on Aging, which was held in Waco, Texas. Other joint efforts at reaching the leadership in the local church and in the convention were also provided. In the area of continuing education, the most effective cooperative venture has been the Summer Institute on Aging for Religious Workers (SIRW). The SIRW is an interfaith offering for all religious groups committed to developing ministries with older persons. It is based on the assumption that all religious organizations need personnel who can assume leadership in the design and implementation of ministry arrangements which touch the physical, emotional, social, and spiritual needs of a diverse and growing aging population. The intention of Baylor's Institute of Gerontological Studies and Southwestern Seminary was to provide participants with the essential knowledge and skills they need to address ministry opportunities and challenges of later life in a more responsive, creative manner. The SIRW consists of two summer sessions. Between these two sessions, the participants make application of what they have learned to ministry arrangements within their religious organizations. The first session (Phase I) is a two-week experience planned by faculty of the Institute of Gerontological Studies. Phase II is held the following summer and is planned by faculty at Southwestern Seminary. Participants who successfully complete the two summer programs of the Institute receive a credential which attests to their achievement.

The curriculum of the Summer Institute on Aging for Religious Workers reflects the multidisciplinary nature of gerontological education and the relevance of this knowledge for ministry with a total person. The content of the first summer session gives focus to the participants' understanding of what productive aging is and the necessary support and encouragement required to achieve this reality. Examples of the content areas for the first summer session include: the physiological changes of aging; policies and programs in aging;

wellness in later life; the law and the elderly; nutritional challenges of later life; aging and mental health; preparation for retirement; computer science implications for aging ministry; and economics and aging. Within each content area, the instructor highlights the implications of the topic for effective ministry with older persons. During the second summer session, content focuses on the development and implementation of ministry approaches within religious organizations. The participants draw on the expertise of a faculty which is uniquely qualified to discuss the translation of gerontological knowledge to the "real world" context of the local church and synagogue. The participants have the opportunity to report on the project they completed during the period between the first and summer sessions.

Based on the mutually beneficial exchanges which have occurred between the two faculties at Baylor and Southwestern Seminary, plans to strengthen the complementary relationship are being made. One area for future development is the intensification of the schedule of faculty exchanges in which Baylor professors offer gerontology courses on the campus of Southwestern Seminary and Southwestern Seminary professors offer courses in ministry with older persons on Baylor's campus. At present, the primary restriction on this exchange program is economic. Both institutions are exploring possible resources for funding this exchange program on a regular basis. Currently, a faculty task force is structuring a plan for a "cooperative degree plan" arrangement between the two institutions. The course sequencing and availability issues are being addressed as well as financial concerns between the institutions. When this task force recommendation is approved, a student will be able to receive a graduate degree from both the Seminary and Baylor University in one year less than would be required without the agreement.

Future plans also include the establishment of a newsletter for religious leaders. This newsletter would be an interfaith offering which would allow the facilities of the two institutions to reach out and provide information that would be helpful to persons directly involved in ministry with the elderly. Some discussion about producing instructional videotapes that could be sent out without charge to religious organizations has also been discussed. These videotapes could be a source of updating information on aging and would be updated to maintain their currency with the field.

As a result of this working agreement, both institutions would like to become more effective in influencing denominational policy and programs as they impact the elderly. This influence would relate to all aspects of denominational life: from the Annuity Board to the various departments that are responsible for the printing of Sunday School literature and other kinds of printed matter, as well as action programs that help the church establish itself at the local level. Currently there is no office on aging within the Southern Baptist Convention, even though there are a number of agencies and departments in these agencies that have an interest in the elderly. Using the influence which they can express individually, as well as collectively, both institutions are committed to a denomination which places a high priority on ministry to and with older persons.

CONTRIBUTORY FACTORS IN MAINTAINING A VIABLE RELATIONSHIP BETWEEN THE UNIVERSITY AND SEMINARY

Three key factors have been operative in maintaining the six-year University-Seminary relationship. It is important that the faculty of the University involved in the cooperative relationship have a substantial interest in and commitment to the role of religion in the aging process. It is this fundamental interest which will motivate university faculty to expend resources in maintaining this "loosely coupled" relationship. In like manner, faculty of the Seminary must be supportive of the academy's involvement in the education of the seminarian. This shared interest is the primary force for the kind of productive relationship which will benefit the older person within religious organizations.

Having established a shared interest, communication among the faculty involved in the relationship is essential in establishing common ground for the cooperative agreement, as well as staking out areas which remain in the individual institution's purview and are not part of the cooperative agreement. Another factor is the importance of the faculty viewing each other on an equal basis. There must be a respect for the scholastic and institutional standards of each institution. This spirit of mutual respect coupled with a shared interest are key ingredients in a workable relationship.

Lastly, there needs to be an appreciation for what each member of the relationship offers the other. For example, a relationship with a seminary provides credibility for the university which seeks to become involved in the area of religion and aging. In like manner, the university is able to cross denominational lines and involve itself with research and programmatic innovations generated by other groups. Thus, the university can be an agent of cross-fertilization between denominations and religious groups, which ultimately benefits the older person within the church and synagogue.

ISSUES
IN THE UNIVERSITY-SEMINARY RELATIONSHIP

While the benefits and successes of the Seminary-University relationship have been documented, issues have emerged during the process which need to be addressed so that those contemplating this type of relationship will be aware of the inherent complexities. One reality is that faculty members at the cooperating institutions already have full-time commitments in their present positions. Essentially, what the cooperative agreement means is that they are asked to assume further responsibilities in implementing its objectives. The faculty of the University setting did not always fully understand the limitations of the Seminary faculty because the University faculty were given the opportunity to work full-time in gerontology and did not have to divide their time with other areas of specialization. For example, one of the key faculty actors in the agreement is also a nationally/internationally known adult educator who has published extensively in this area and is in high demand for conferences. With these demands, he must also find ways of allocating time for maintaining the agreement. Another issue is that of budgetary limitations. As was mentioned when discussing the faculty exchange program, the budgetary implications of establishing the agreement must carefully be considered if all of its provisions are to be implemented. In times of economic scarcity, this limitation can effectively curtail full implementation of the agreement. As the agreement was implemented within the institutions, it was noted that many faculty are not prepared to be involved with aging studies. For some, there is a lack of sensitivity to the impact of this population on religious organizations and for others, this lack of interest may reflect a type of gerontophobia. Whatever the reason, considerable effort may be required in getting the gerontology innovation adopted within courses.

A very difficult issue faced by the participants in the agreement centered on the mechanics for crediting students for the work they performed at the University and the Seminary. Part of this issue related the unfortunate reality of elitism within the university setting. At times there appears to be a tendency to think that seminary training is not at the same academic level as graduate education in the university. Consequently, there is a reluctance to transfer hours of seminary credit to the university graduate degree. In this case study, the participating Seminary was much more willing to accept University graduate credit. There has to be more understanding on the part of university faculty concerning the purposes of seminary education, the demands of the curriculum, and the qualifications of the faculty so that greater equity may be possible in the relationship.

The challenges of developing cooperative degree programs are numerous. For precise academic planning, each institution must be able to provide the other with course offerings which correlate with the degree requirements as well as the kind of scheduling which will meet the demands of seminary and university students who must travel in order to participate in the course. Faculty must be motivated to continue with the cooperative agreement and it is helpful when they can be provided with some incentive to maintain their level of involvement. Faculty who implement the agreement should work hard to instill a sense of ownership in the cooperative program. Complicating the relationship between faculty is the possibility of competition. It is very easy for two schools to compete without fully being aware of it and, therefore, it is important that faculty are careful to affirm their colleagues and focus on the strengths which they bring to the relationship. Another factor which sometimes contributes to a low responsiveness in the seminary setting is the small number of churches which hire senior adult ministers. Often, Southern Baptist churches rely on lay leadership and/or some combination with another paid staff to meet the needs of their older members. As long as the demand for senior adult ministers is at a low level, it will be difficult to entice seminarians into involvement with gerontological education. These issues as well as others present the challenges to maintaining an effective reciprocal relationship.

CONCLUSIONS

This case study demonstrated the potential of a university and seminary working together to develop a cooperative program in gerontological education for religious leaders. Paramount in this working relationship is a strong commitment on the part of both institutions to share their resources freely with the other, acknowledge the quality of each other's roles, and share a similar vision as to the need of such training for ministry. Factors which contribute to the success of this programmatic arrangement include: the endorsement of the chief administrator; shared denominational identity; previous experience of gerontology faculty and staff at each institution; willingness to take risks and accept failure; and finally, the joint appreciation of the need of such cooperation to provide gerontological education. The majority of the issues identified have been addressed and only a few remain, such as increasing faculty participation, administrative support within the seminary setting, and integrating gerontological education in the curriculum of students majoring in such areas as theology and music. Therefore, the future holds great promise in that similar relationships are being initiated by Baylor with other Southern Baptist seminaries. Hopefully, the consequences of this expanded network will be a more informed approach to aging by churches throughout the country and the world.

Six implications can be drawn from the experience presented in this case study.

1. The university-seminary relationship maximizes gerontological educational opportunities and resources available and minimizes the economic cost of producing these resources.
2. The possibility of duplication of courses offered at each institution is minimized.
3. Students can earn degrees at each institution in a time period

one year shorter than a student would experience if the degrees were offered separately. This is an obvious benefit to the student and ultimately expedites the delivery of ministry services to older persons.

4. The relationship increases the visibility of aging ministries within the denomination and provides a vehicle for influencing denominational policy and priority setting.

5. The seminarian and university student are provided with opportunities to consider career options which would otherwise not be available to them outside of the cooperative arrangement.

6. The instructional and research capability of the university and seminary are combined in a manner which contributes to a multidisciplinary understanding of the aging experience.

On the basis of the six-year experience in the cooperative relationship, and after consideration of the implications mentioned, the authors recommend that other cooperative agreements be given consideration by higher education administration and faculty who are interested in realizing the benefits of this type of reciprocal relationship.

PART 3:
AN ANNOTATED BIBLIOGRAPHY

The annotated bibliography has been developed to serve as a guide for acquiring basic library holdings on gerontology and on religion and aging. It is intended for use by theological seminaries, by colleges and universities with joint relationships with seminaries, and by those institutions including religion in their gerontological curriculum.

Most of the religion and aging materials are relatively recent, but there are some historical materials which are important in understanding present practice. Since attention to aging is a recent phenomenon, seminary libraries will need to purchase retrospectively and be intentional in the collection of particular works which might otherwise be lost.

Converse to the seminary library situation, most other institutions with gerontology programs have limited holdings on religion and aging and their libraries will need to add to their gerontological collections. This annotated bibliography is intended to be useful for such acquisitions.

Gerontology and Religion:
An Annotated Bibliography

Barbara Payne, PhD

SUMMARY. This annotated bibliography provides resources for librarians in theological schools and in gerontology programs. It is divided into two sections: (1) Gerontology and Applied Practices; and (2) Theological Disciplines and Clergy Practices. A careful review of these useful annotations should guide the acquisition of significant materials for programs in religion and gerontology.

This bibliography differs in its primary focus from other annotated bibliographies dealing with religion and aging, such as Fecher (1982) and Cook (1976) in its primary focus on institutional library resources for religious professionals. The focus is on institutional library resources. It includes books and journals which should be valuable in program development for gerontology in theological education and religion in gerontological curriculum.

The bibliography is divided into two sections: (1) Gerontology and Applied Practices and (2) Theological Disciplines and Clergy Practices.

The first section includes introductory and background works in gerontology as a multidisciplinary field of study, research and practice; materials on physical and biological aspects; psychological works related to personality, the self/ego, life stage development, cognition, reminiscence, depression, mental health etc.; and social gerontology selections on family and intergenerational relation-

Barbara Payne is Director of the Gerontology Center, Georgia State University. Staff members include Virginia Erhardt, Catherine Healey, MSW, Mary MacKinnon, MN, Barbara Thompson, MDiv, MS. Other contributors include Henry Simmons, PhD, and Earl D. C. Brewer, PhD.

ships, political and policy issues, the humanities, health and welfare, economics, retirement, older workers, volunteerism, leisure, consumer markets, and social problems including crime, drugs, elder abuse, housing, and transportation.

The second section, Theological Disciplines and Clergy Practices, is made up of two parts: (1) materials to relate aging to theology, Biblical studies, history and tradition, ethics, religious education, and faith development; and (2) works relating aging to the theological practices of pastoral care and counseling, preaching, speech and communication, congregational programs, evangelism and outreach.

Books included in the required reading lists of syllabi submitted in the research project are identified by an asterisk, "*" and additional works evaluated as most significant by a double asterisk, "**" in the following annotated bibliography.

GERONTOLOGY AND APPLIED PRACTICES

1. Achenbaum, W. Old Age in the New Land: The American Experience Since 1970. Baltimore, MD: The Johns Hopkins University Press, 1978.

This remarkable classic study explores the roots of our cultural attitudes toward aging. Old age is viewed as a special time in life with its own set of roles, status, perceptions, and realities. In spite of living in a new, rich land, old age is viewed with a deep-seated fear and aversion. Achenbaum makes use of historical data and cultural analysis to show that ageist attitudes and practices are the result of an interweaving of many factors over time and not just due to a rapidly growing older population or simple stereotyping of older persons as non-productive, dependent, and poor. The new programs of the 1970s are seen as a way to impact positively these deep-rooted negative attitudes of an ageist society.

2. * Atchley, R.C. Social Forces and Aging (Fifth Edition). Belmont, CA: Wadsworth, 1988.

The fifth edition of the first major social gerontology text continues Atchley's tradition of providing a comprehensive, readable and relevant introduction to social gerontology for undergraduates as well as graduates. Many sections and chapters have been heavily revised. New sections have been added on social policy, emotions, professional practice, politics of social security, age stratification, elder hostel, sleep, and home care, with an emphasis on integration of theoretical approaches.

3. Bengtson, V.L. & Robertson, J.F. (Eds.). Grandparenthood. Beverly Hills, CA: Sage Publications, 1985.

This volume of contributed chapters attempts to bring together multiple perspectives on both traditional and emergent aspects of grandparenthood. The two essays in Part IV on "Grandparents and Religion," and "The Context of Values" are of specific interest to pastors, rabbis, seminary students, religious educators, and social workers. The contributed essays provide information and insight into intergenerational relations and significant implications for communal and pastoral programs to enhance the well-being of intergenerational families.

4. * Billig, N. To Be Old and Sad: Understanding Depression in the Elderly. Lexington, MA: D.C. Heath, 1987.

A geriatric psychiatrist provides a practical, supportive work geared to families with older members. The volume is also addressed to older adults who are concerned about depression in themselves, in friends, and in family members and who want to learn more about its origins, symptoms and treatment. It is an excellent source for those, such as the clergy, who are in the helping professions.

5. Binstock, R.H. & Shanas, E. Handbook of Aging and the Social Sciences (Second Edition). New York: Van Nostrand Reinhold, 1985.

The purposes of this Handbook are to provide comprehensive information, major reference sources, and central issues for further research in aging, from the systemic perspectives of a variety of social sciences. Forty authors and co-authors are "top echelon specialists in their respective subject areas." The 26 chapters are organized in five major sections: I. The Study Of Aging; II. The Social Aspects of Aging; III. Aging and Social Structure; IV. Aging and Social Systems; and V. Aging and Social Intervention. Religion is included in Chapter 5 as one of the historical perceptions of age. Religion and religious institutions are not included in the other chapters on social science and practices.

6. Birren, J.E. & Bengtson, V.L. (Eds.). Emerging Theories of Aging. New York: Springer, 1988.

This volume is an attempt by researchers to address "data-rich but theory poor" research on aging and to encourage cross-disciplinary interchange on theory development. The book is divided into four parts: Part I addresses the bases of theory building in aging; Part II examines biological theories in aging and implications for the behavioral and social sciences; Part III reviews psychological concepts and theories of aging; and, Part IV is devoted to social science concepts and theories of aging. The volume reflects the multidisciplinary nature of gerontology but does not propose a grand macro, multidisciplinary theory. The contributed chapters provide an overview of theories for interpreting and designing aging research by faculty and graduate students in theology and gerontology.

7. Birren, J.E. & Schaie, K.W. (Eds.). Handbook of the Psychology of Aging (Second Edition). New York: Van Nostrand Reinhold, 1985.

The purpose of the Handbook is to provide "an authoritative review and definitive reference source of the scientific and professional literature on the psychological and behavioral aspects of aging for students, researchers, and professionals. The basic behavioral processes from primary sensory phenomena to personality and behavioral disorders and changes are described and explained by the various contributors from specialized areas of psychology." There is no reference to religion or belief systems in any of the chapters including subjective well-being.

8. Breytspraak, L. The Development of Self in Later Life. Boston: Little, Brown & Company, 1984.

This volume is a systematic survey of what we know about self processes and aging. The author's work is based on two assumptions: the self is a useful organizing concept for understanding the individual's confrontation with the aging processes and that the self can continue to develop throughout the life course. The author reviews psychological, sociological and gerontological theoretical traditions and interests in issues of selfhood, discusses mechanisms used to negotiate, manage, and maintain a viable sense of self, examines "how older people both respond to and actively manage and negotiate their self conceptualizations and evaluations as they come to terms with their finitude, their achievements and failures, their changing bodies, the images and stereotypes of old age that pervade the larger society, and a changing constellation of social roles." The religious professional interested in spiritual growth and personal development of older persons will find this book has practical as well as theoretical significance.

9. * Brubaker, T.H. (Ed.). Family Relationships in Later Life. Beverly Hills, CA: Sage Publications, 1983.

This volume of collected works is a review of research on issues of sexuality, sex roles, widowhood, divorce, abuse, minority issues and family relationships in later life. It also includes suggestions for practice and further research. Divided into three sections: Part I considers specific relationships of older persons such as husband-wife, parent-child, sibling, grandparent; Part II focuses on a number of issues related to the later-life family; Part III focuses on policy and practices aspects. The research-based understanding of later-life families provides valuable, non-jargon information needed by the religious professional to understand the issues facing older families.

10. * Brubaker, T.H. Later Life Families. Beverly Hills, CA: Sage Publications, 1985.

The primary focus of this book is on families who have progressed to the later stages of the family life cycle and are dealing with the tasks associated with later life. Based on the assumption that the later life family is alive and well, it examines and integrates the research to support this contention. Topics include long-term marriages, relationships with adult children and their families, remarriage, support services to older persons and their families, the older person's position as spouse, parent, sibling and grandparent.

11. * Butler, R.N. Why Survive? Being Old in America. New York: Harper & Row, 1975.

This Pulitzer Prize winning book portrays realistically the experience of older people in the United States in the early 1970s. It makes an appeal to rationality and examines public policy toward the elderly. Although some statistics have changed as the author predicted, this book remains a major useful source and resource for the 1980s and beyond. The examination includes the consequences of age segregation — of young or old, the devalued view of older persons, and negative stereotypes. Butler introduces the concepts of ageism, life review and reminiscence. Religion in old age and the role of religious institutions are interwoven throughout the volume.

12. Butler, R.N. & Lewis, M.I. Aging and Mental Health: Positive Psychosocial and Biological Approaches (Third Edition). St. Louis: C.V. Mosby, 1982.

The third edition describes some of the progress in mental health care for older people. Additions include new demographical and biometric data, developments in the neurosciences, the growth of information in the psychopharmacology of old age, and a discussion of the newest classifications of mental disorders. The field has been expanded to include positive psychological and biomedical approaches. It includes some current major problems, both in bringing quality mental health care to older people and in creating an environment that promotes mental health. The authors include a short but significant section on religious support for older persons. The clergy are described as one of the few professional disciplines whose members are trained to care for dying people and give special attention to older members. They recommend a practical "ecumenism" which would allow churches and synagogues to protect their identities yet pool their resources in a planned effort to help older people.

13. ** Butler, R.N. & Lewis, M.L. Sex After Sixty. New York: Harper & Row, 1976.

This volume is a guide for older men and women and for younger people who want to know what their future holds for them sexually. It includes chapters on normal physical changes in sex and sexuality with age; common medical and emotional problems related to sex; learning new patterns of love-making; those with no partners, dating, remarriage, sons and daughters, and where to go for help. The chapter on the second language of love is a classic, creative contribution.

14. ** Callahan, D. Setting Limits: Medical Goals in an Aging Society. New York: Simon & Schuster, 1987.

The director/co-founder of The Hastings Center, nationally renowned for its work in the field of medical ethics, has already sparked debate and is destined to affect public policy. The controversy centers on Callahan's interpretation of increased longevity as a socio-economic health care issue. He starts with Butler's question, why survive growing old? and raises the questions, but is it affordable? and at what expense to the young? He proposes limitations to health care and treatment of the elderly. The development of the implications of these basic issues are divided into a discussion of how, in the light of medical progress, should we understand aging? (Chapter 2); given the potential of an unending medical struggle against aging and death, is there an alternate more suitable goal? (Chapter 3); what are the obligations of the young toward the old, personally and socially, and the obligations of the old to the young? (Chapter 6); and finally the question of intergenerational obligation. These are bold suggested solutions to problems and issues that are not going away in the foreseeable future. These are ethical issues that need to be addressed in religious ethics classes.

15. ** Chambree, S.M. & Pollack, O. Good Deeds in Old Age: Volunteering by the New Leisure Class. Lexington, MA: Lexington Press, 1987.

This book is based on the secondary analysis of data collected by Lou Harris and Associates for a survey sponsored by the National Council on the Aging. Each of the 11 chapters includes a review of and inclusion of relevant literature on the following topics: the role of volunteering in older people's lives; research methods; volunteering as a role substitute in widowhood and retirement; age and health status; socio-economic status and the costs and rewards of volunteering; the diminishing importance of gender, race and religion; older persons as joiners; life satisfaction; expanding volunteering by older people.

16. * Clements, W.M. Care and Counseling of the Aging. Philadelphia: Fortress Press, 1979.

The unique feature of this volume is the therapeutic use of reminiscence in pastoral care and counseling. The emphasis on getting in touch with our feelings about our own aging has practical and personal application for all religious professionals.

17. Cohen, D. & Eisdorfer, C. The Loss of Self: A Family Resource for the Care of Alzheimer's Disease and Related Disorders. New York: Penguin, 1986.

Based on over 15 years of research and clinical experience, this volume interprets that experience in the form of presenting options, understanding and caring for patient and caregiver, as a guide to recognizing when memory problems are serious, where to get evaluations, etc. Clergy will find this volume helpful in ministering to families with an Alzheimer's Disease patient, and interpreting this problem to the local congregation.

18. Cole, T.R. & Gadow, S.A. (Eds.). What Does It Mean to Grow Old? Reflections from the Humanities. Durham, NC: Duke, 1986.

Prominent scholars from various disciplines of the humanities (philosophy, history, theology, sociology, law) reflect on the meaning of aging and death. These humanistic perspectives allow them to grasp some profoundly human aspects of aging which have an openness to religious life.

19. Coleman, P.G. Aging and Reminiscence Processes: Social and Clinical Implications. New York: John Wiley & Sons, 1986.

This volume is based on a fifteen-year longitudinal study of the lives, attitudes toward reminiscence of older people living alone in sixteen sheltered housing sites in the London area. The sample included 27 women and 23 men with an average age of 80. The author, a clinical psychologist, describes in detail his open-ended methods and the use of six questionnaires. Chapters 1-4 are an introduction to the study and the subjects. Chapters 5-9 contain the main body of the work and use case studies as examples of the aspect of reminiscence discussed. The topical areas include: valuing memories; regret and resolution; no point in looking back; loss and depression; and toward integrity. The final chapter is devoted to therapeutic implications. The seminary faculty, students and clergy will find the method useful in working with older persons and the application of religious faith to these areas which brings a new understanding of the spiritual life of older adults.

20. Couper, D.P. Aging and Our Families: A Handbook for Family Caregivers. Washington, DC: Administration on Aging, 1987.

This handbook was developed as a part of the Caregiver Information Project funded by the Administration on Aging as a joint effort of the Travelers Center on Aging, University of Connecticut and the State of Connecticut, Department on Aging. The guide book is a valuable resource for developing programs and ministry for and with older persons and their families in local congregations. The focus is on the primary caregiver in families and suggests practical ways to strengthen support systems for them among friends, neighbors and through religious and community groups. The guide is divided into three parts: Part I describes and discusses the situation of aging from the perspective of the family caregiver. It includes activities to aid in understanding the situation; Part II focuses on understanding relationships in the caregiving situation and includes activities to help caregivers understand the interdependence of these relationships; Part III gives an overview of common decision making problems and possible alternatives. Practical guides for making decisions are included.

21. * Coward, R.T. & Lee, G.R. (Eds.). The Elderly in Rural Society. New York: Springer, 1985.

This is Volume 13 in the Springer Series on Adulthood and Aging. The editors and sixteen contributors provide a substantial review of rural elders in the United States. Every fourth elderly person (59 million) lives in a rural area. In almost every aspect of life (low income, substandard housing, more health problems, more alcohol problems, inadequate physical and mental health facilities and less public transportation) rural elderly fare less well than their urban counterparts. The contributions of this volume deal with research into these and related issues and suggestions for improving the lot of older persons living in rural America.

22. * Cox, H.G. Later Life: The Realities of Aging (Second Edition). Englewood Cliffs, NJ: Prentice-Hall, 1988.

This second edition of a basic text in gerontology reflects the interdisciplinary nature of the subject and includes material from psychology, sociology, social work, anthropology, the biological sciences, medicine and psychiatry. Included is a well organized chapter on religion and aging that integrates socio-psychological religious studies with limited works from gerontology and religion. A timely section on elder abuse is also included.

23. Cumming, E. & Henry, W.E. Growing Old: The Process of Disengagement. New York: Basic Books, 1961.

This is a classic in gerontology and documents the introduction of the theory of disengagement. Based on a major empirical study, it is one of the first attempts to interpret the social and psychological nature of the aging process in American society. It remains useful in understanding transitions in roles and adaptation to retirement.

24. de Beauvoir, S. The Coming of Age. New York: G. P. Putnam's Sons, 1972.

This classic work gives a clarion call to look at how society views old age. De Beauvoir is determined to give voice to the real work of aging and to break the "conspiracy of silence" that relegates old people to the status of non-persons, marginal, poor, dependent, outcasts. She calls us to acceptance of the reality of aging as the only way to approach the future with personal integrity and purpose. Meaning is found in living out the process of aging. Part One covers the biological, anthropological, historical, and sociological views of aging. Part Two focuses on the personal response to aging in relation to the body, time, and the outside world.

25. Dunkle, R.E., Houg, M.E. & Rosenberg, M. (Eds.). Communications Technology and the Elderly. New York: Springer, 1984.

This book of contributed chapters addresses two types of technology: devices to improve hearing and sight of aged persons and mechanisms to link the elderly with health care delivery systems, marketing and recreational systems.

Part I brings together the views of an engineer and a biomedical specialist who stress the implications of their specialties for the quality of life. Part II defines the older person's communication needs from the perspective of a development psychologist and a sociologist. Part III explains the utility of devices to correct low-vision problems and the uses of various types of hearing aids for the elderly. Parts IV and V describe the diverse ways of connecting older persons with services and the potential market for communication devices. The use of technology by which to improve communication with the elderly impacts the effectiveness of congregational programing for the elderly.

26. ** Erikson, E.H. The Life Cycle Completed: A Review. New York: W.W. Norton, 1982.

This volume is essentially the author's invited essay for the National Institute of Mental Health three-volume set, *The Course of Life: Psychoanalytic Contributions Toward Understanding Personality Development*. The major change, based on his own aging, is to begin with adulthood, not childhood. Erikson argues that once you have worked out the interweaving of all stages you should be able to start with any stage and meaningfully reach any other on the map of stages. He stresses the recent discovery of "old age" and a mass of "elderlies" rather than "elite elders." The discoveries about human growth and development in late life by this elite developmental psychologist is significant to those who serve predominately adult and elderly congregations.

27. ** Erikson, E.H., Erikson, J.M. & Kivnick, H.Q. Vital Involvement in Old Age. New York: W.W. Norton, 1986.

E.H. Erikson's eight stages of the life cycle provide the theoretical framework for the authors to interpret the last stage — old age. The emphasis is on the continual involvements necessary at each stage. The life-historical perspective is applied to a sample of older age-specific people in a specific time period. The empirical base is the interviews with the survivors who were the child participants in the Berkley Guidance Study (1929). The major portion of the book, Part II "The Voices of Our Informants" identifies and interprets from the life experience of octogenarians a psychosocial process of vital involvement from infancy to old age. The stages are reversed, the sections begin with the new description of Erikson's eighth stage as Integrity vs. Despair: Wisdom. One section reports on the role of religion and faith in late life. It confirms and contradicts many of the popular and research views of religion and aging.

28. Finch, C.E. & Schneider, E.L. The Handbook of the Biology of Aging (Second Edition). New York: Van Nostrand Reinhold, 1985.

The second edition updates and extends the 1978 edition with mostly different authors and many new topics. This volume provides the non-biologist with the most current review of the interrelationships between aging and disease and the emerging field of geriatric medicine. Perspectives on aging and mortality, nutrition and aging, and health maintenance and longevity provide religious professionals and faculty with basic biological practice resources.

29. ** Fisher, D.H. Growing Old in America. New York: Oxford Press, 1978.

This is one of the first comprehensive efforts of an historian to research the history of old age. Fisher's purposes are: to describe and discuss the context of old age as a system of age relations which embraces everyone according to his chronological condition; to establish the mainlines of change, its pattern, pace and timing; to locate primary pieces of evidence that bear upon aging; and to put the pieces together in a coherent way. The table of contents demonstrates the historian's ability to apply historical methods and evidence to give new insights for understanding aging in American society. These are: The Gerontogratia: The Exaltation of Age in Early America, 1607-1820; Transition: The Revolution in Age Relations, 1770-1820; Gerontophobia: The Cult of Youth in Modern America, 1770-1970; Transition: Old Age Becomes a Social Problem, 1909-1970; and Gerontophratria: A Thought for the Future, 1909- . The influence of religion on age relations is one of the major pieces of evidence.

30. Gray, R.H. Survival of the Spirit: My Detour Through a Retirement Home. Atlanta: John Knox Press, 1984.

Excerpts from a diary written in a woman's 85th year of struggle to maintain her individuality and personhood in a retirement home in the face of inflexible and insensitive administrations. The author and her peers emerge as positive, creative, but embattled people. Her experience should increase understanding of the retired or institutionalized older adult.

31. Gubrium, F. Living and Dying at Murray Manor. New York: St. Martin's Press, 1975.

This window on daily life and work in a nursing home is a classic study of all facets of place, staff, residents, and patients that constitute the social organization and structure of Murray Manor. In spite of societal stereotyping about nursing home residents, which has some real reflection at Murray Manor, the social fabric of life there is as complex and as ordinary as that of any other group who share their lives regularly. This study examines the details of daily living and work, including relationships, roles, status, rights, duties and needs of the staff and clientele and their private and corporate domains.

32. Harris, D.K., Palmore, E.B. & Stanley, S.C. Teaching Sociology of Aging. Washington, DC: ASA Teaching Resource Center, 1722 N Street, Washington, DC 20036, 1986.

This is a practical working document for courses or modules related to the sociological aspects of aging. The introduction is a helpful essay for preparing a course; Chapter 1 is a collection of syllabi from 48 distinguished social gerontologists which covers a wide range of substantive sociological areas. Chapter 2 presents helpful teaching techniques; Chapter 3 has exercises and student paper assignments; Chapter 4 introduces reading lists collected from sociologists and recommended films; and, Chapter 5 has a collection of examinations.

33. Hendricks, J. & Hendricks, C.D. Aging in Mass Society: Myths and Reality (Third Edition). Boston: Little, Brown & Company, 1986.

This third edition of a multidisciplinary text for gerontology courses is markedly different from the two previous ones. In addition to deletions and reorganization of material, a new chapter on Social Policy and Aging has been added. The purpose of the text is to provide a holistic and comprehensive description of the dimensions of aging. Part One is an introduction to the field of gerontology; Part Two summarizes what we know of the lifeworld of the aging person; Part Three contains a societal view of aging and context of aging including social context effects on older persons. Chapter 11 on social policy issues is an excellent resource for courses in social ethics and modules dealing with the applied aspects of ministry or advocacy for the elderly. Part Four attempts to forecast the future for the elderly, society and those interested in careers in gerontology.

34. Herr, J.J. & Weakland, J.H. Counseling Elders and Their Families. New York: Springer, 1979.

As our society ages, we are becoming sophisticated enough to know that growing old is not always a problem. Many older adults are having the time of their lives, while unfortunately others have problems of health, income, and loneliness. This book directly addresses these problems in the context of the family, because the affairs of an aging person are family affairs.

One of the issues explored by the authors is the dynamics of guilt and communication within interfamily relations, which can place limitations on the kinds of solutions that are possible. Herr and Weakland give a format for approaching the problem of older adults in the family context. This book is a provocative and useful tool for helping counselors to perceive how they can be more effective in counseling family members.

35. Kaminsky, M. The Uses of Reminiscence: New Ways of Working with Older Adults. New York: Haworth Press, 1984.

This special issue of the *Journal of Gerontological Social Work* presents a coherent and sophisticated conceptual understanding of reminiscence. Several essays illustrate a variety of practical approaches for using reminiscence individually and in groups to help participants accomplish a level of meaning which is personally integrative and socially critical.

36. ** Kaufman, S.R. The Ageless Self: Sources of Meaning in Late Life. New York: New American Library, 1986.

This volume is based on a study of aging through the expression of individual humanity by 60 older Americans. These persons were not found to perceive meaning in aging itself; rather, they perceived meaning in being themselves in old age. They expressed a sense of self that is ageless—an identity that maintains continuity despite the physical and social changes of life. The 60 life-story tellers focus on what was meaningful in their past and how they describe themselves in old age. Themes in the life-stories are identified, as are the structural sources of meaning and values in later life. The qualitative methodology is applicable to the study of older Americans and religious life.

37. Kelly, J.R. Peoria Winter: Styles and Resources in Later Life. Lexington, MA: D.C. Heath, Lexington Books, 1987.

This research study reports how older persons have dealt with the continuities and discontinuities of their life course. Findings are based on the life course as a process that involves cumulative development of resources, responses, and deprivations in relation to the inevitability of change. Kelly identifies three life course types and nine styles of coping as indicative of passage through the life course. Those who cope best tend to be persons who invest themselves in at least two of the life domains of family, work, leisure, and community. They are also persons who have found a sense of direction that impels them into life rather than resigning them to an uncertain fate.

38. Kotre, J. Outliving the Self. Baltimore, MD: Johns Hopkins University Press, 1984.

This work describing the development of a theory of generativity, modified from Erikson, includes biological, parental, technical and cultural dimensions. It is then applied to the stories of four women and four men, not all of them elderly.

39. Lesnoff-Caravaglia, G. (Ed.). Handbook of Applied Gerontology. New York: Human Sciences Press, 1987.

This handbook is an interdisciplinary collaboration and contribution of 31 gerontologists. The three sections represent major areas of concern about aging individuals: (1) the physical self; (2) personal adaptation and mental health in old age; and (3) social realities of old age issues of individual choice and dependency. These sections reflect a life span perspective and the common theme of prevention and intervention. This handbook provides excellent resources for practitioners, researchers and academicians.

40. Lesnoff-Caravaglia, G. (Ed.). Values, Ethics and Aging. New York: Human Sciences Press, 1985.

This volume is a collection of essays on the humanities and aging by 16 contributors. They seek to demonstrate the contribution that humanists may add to the understanding of the social and psychological aspects of aging. In addition to five essays on religion, the contributors address values, ethical, political and legal issues as well as historical perspectives.

41. Litwak, E. Helping the Elderly: The Contemporary Roles of Informal Networks and Formal Systems. New York: The Guilford Press, 1985.

This book is an answer to the question "which groups are best suited to provide which services to older people?" The answer involves a theoretical perspective combined with survey research to demonstrate how formal organizations can collaborate with primary groups in meeting the needs of the elderly. Litwak demonstrates the principle that groups can optimally manage those tasks that match them in structure. This principle explains which services older people will receive uniquely from neighbors, friends, spouses, and kin. The same principle of matching is applied to formal organizations such as nursing homes to show which sorts of services nursing homes can take over from primary groups. The principle of matching is applied to neighborhood structure including local clubs and voluntary organizations. The church or synagogue or church-connected groups are subsumed under this analysis. It is left up to the religious professional to apply the principle of matching to the religious organization and its link with primary groups and neighborhoods.

42. ** Maddox, G.L.A. (Editor-in-chief). The Encyclopedia of Aging. New York: Springer, 1987.

This major reference work provides authoritative explanations for hundreds of terms and concepts relating to the life of the elderly and the aging process. Up-to-date and comprehensive, the Encyclopedia includes information on biomedical, psychological, and social topics. It also covers the growing range of programs and services for the elderly provided by the professions, the communities and government agencies. In addition to the five associate editors, Robert C. Atchley, Leonard W. Poon, George S. Roth, Irene C. Siegler and Raymond Steinberg, there are more than 225 distinguished contributors. The Encyclopedia features 500 entries, 8,000 cross-referenced index items, and the most comprehensive bibliography on aging ever compiled.

43. Mangen, D.J. & Peterson, W.A. (Eds.). Research Instruments in Social Gerontology, Volume 1: Clinical and Social Psychology. Minneapolis: University of Minnesota Press, 1982.

This is the first in a three-volume series designed to serve the needs of researchers, evaluators and clinicians in assessing the instruments used in the field of aging. Volume 1 focuses on the cognitive reactions to aging of older people and on the assessments of their own and others' aging made by people who are not yet old. The eleven contributors provide a concise narrative review of the major theoretical concerns and measurement strategies within their research area. Each chapter contains abstracts and, when possible, copies of instruments.

44. Mangen, D.J. & Peterson, W.A. (Eds.). Research Instruments in Social Gerontology, Volume 2: Social Roles and Social Participation. Minneapolis: University of Minnesota Press, 1982.

The measures reviewed in the second of a three-volume series address the concern of social gerontologists with the involvement of older persons in the major forms of social organization and social structure. The 10 contributed chapters deal with areas of special interest to researchers, evaluators and clinicians in the field of religion, such as social participation, roles, dyadic relations, parent-child relations, kinship relations, work and retirement, socio-economic status and poverty, religiosity, friends, neighbors and confidantes, voluntary associations, and leisure activities.

45. Mangen, D.J. & Peterson, W.A. (Eds.). Research Instruments in Social Gerontology, Volume 3: Health, Program Evaluation and Demography. Minneapolis: University of Minnesota Press, 1984.

Volume 3 of the three-volume series differs significantly from Volumes 1 and 2. "Many of the instruments reviewed are not discrete, limited collections of items that purport to measure a single concept." The instruments contain items measuring several concepts not related to health, program evaluation or demography. Only sample items are included. The eleven contributors' topics are: functional capacity; health; utilization of health services; individual needs and community resources; social program tracking and evaluation; the effectiveness of long-term care; evaluating of cost of services; organizational properties; indexes for the aging of populations; demographic characteristics; and geographic mobility.

46. ** Marshall, V.W. (Ed.) Later Life: The Social Psychology of Aging. Beverly Hills, CA: Sage Publications, 1986.

The contributors to this book about theory in social gerontology agree with the goals of the volume: to recognize that aging individuals are embedded in social structural contexts that have their own historical and social imperatives and dynamics; to critique the structural-functionalist approach to social gerontology; and to introduce the basic elements of an interpretative perspective based on Weberian sociology, symbolic interactionist sociology and phenomenological psychology. The contributors approach these goals with a variety of themes such as friendship, death and dying, social networks and social support, and historical review. This work offers theoretical frameworks for interpreting the social aging process and the development of the self in later life.

47. ** Matthews, S. The Social World of Old Women: Management of Self-Identity. Beverly Hills: Sage Publications, 1979.

Based on her research, Matthews provides a "close up" look at the social worlds of older women by clarifying the social forces that impinge on them. If this research account of the everyday life issues that differentiate the experiences of women is read along with Boyle and Parnes et al., the reader may gain a better understanding of unique gender differences in old age.

48. McNeely, R.L. & Colen, J.L. (Editors). Aging in Minority Groups. Beverly Hills: Sage Publications, 1983.

This volume is intended as a comprehensive description of the many dimensions of minority aging. It examines not only the negative aspects of minority aging, but highlights the more favorable aspects. Contributors to this volume address the significant differences existing among and within subpopulations of the aged. The chapters related to a specific minority group were written by members of that group. There are five thematic sections: an introductory review; demographic profiles of the aged in each minority group; the dynamics of aging within three specific cultural groups; selected aging social problems and their impact on minorities; and problems in the delivery of services to minority aged. The increase in the numbers of minority elderly and the dearth of in-depth literature on these subpopulations make this a significant source for religious professionals serving multiethnic communities.

49. Mishara, B.L. & Kastenbaum, R. Alcohol and Old Age. New York: Grune & Stratton, 1980.

This volume brings together the existing body of knowledge concerning alcohol and old age. It presents the conflicting opinions about alcohol being of value in old age and its being dangerous. This effort to find the most accurate view moves from an historical overview to the psychological effects; epidemiological data on usage; methods of treating older alcoholics; to a multidimensional view. This book is a resource for religious professionals who counsel families and older adults about the use and abuse of alcohol in old age.

50. Moberg, D.O. Spiritual Well-Being: Sociological Perspectives. Washington, DC: University Press of America, 1979.

This volume is an edited collection of papers on spiritual well-being delivered by the contributors at two international professional meetings: the Association for the Sociology of Religion, March 1977 and International Sociological Association in Uppsala, Sweden, August 1978. The articles are grouped by conceptual studies; theory, qualitative and quantitative research. Most of the contributions are not age specific, but have implications for aging. The one exception is Earl D.C. Brewers' "Life Stages and Spiritual Well-Being" which reviews life stages' work and presents a new theoretical model.

51. Monk, A. (Ed.). Handbook of Gerontological Services. New York: Van Nostrand Reinhold, 1985.

This handbook is written from a practice perspective and intended for a wide range of professional, academic, student and non-professional users. There are three types of services covered: services in high demand and widely used, specialized services, and those that are meeting needs now but will be more important in the future. The handbook deals with "state-of-the-art" practice as well as the diversity of views about services prevalent in the field of gerontology. The book addresses: Concepts and Issues, Client Evaluation, Treatment and Intervention Modalities, Community-Based Services, Home-Based Services, Long-Term Care and Institution-Based Services, and Policy, Planning and Operation of Services. This handbook contains a wealth of resources.

52. Moore, P. Disguised. Waco, TX: Word Books, 1985.

This true story of a young woman who journeyed into the world of an old woman presents a picture of life in this country for older persons in the late 1970s and early 1980s. With the aid of professional makeup, prostheses, ear plugs, joints taped to limit movement, and other paraphernalia, Pat Moore became a woman of 80 + for three years. She developed three characters for her research effort: a wealthy woman, a middle income woman, and a poor "bag lady." This participant-observation research technique was used with care and integrity in 116 cities, 14 states, and 2 Canadian provinces, to allow the author, as an industrial designer and student of gerontology, to discover ways to create products that would allow older persons to control their environment with mastery and dignity regardless of disabilities. She found that myths and stereotypes of aging are insidious and indeed permeate our society making life difficult. She makes a plea for creating a new intergenerational world and offers some guidelines, beginning with the education of children, about aging.

53. ** Morris, W.W. & Bader, I.M. (Eds.). Hoffman's Daily Needs and Interests of Older People (Second Edition). Springfield, IL: Charles C Thomas, 1983.

This second edition reflects the changes in needs and interests of older persons occurring between 1970 and 1983. These changes are incorporated in the contributed chapters which deal with problems encountered by all older people regardless of their backgrounds or present situations. These needs include: nutrition, housing, economic security, health, clothing, leisure, and family relationships. There are two chapters on religion that discuss the role of religion in the later years and the impact of religion and bereavement in old age.

54. Murguia, E., Schulz, T.M., Markides, K.S. & Janson, P. (Compilers). Ethnicity and Aging: A Bibliography. San Antonio, TX: Trinity University Press, 1984.

This volume is a "comprehensive but selective" multiethnic bibliography on American aging. The primary and secondary works are divided into seven sections: multiethnic and general studies; black Americans; Hispanic Americans; native Americans; Asian and Pacific Americans; European origin ethnic groups; and other bibliographies. Each section is divided into topical areas which include religion, death and dying, leisure, marriage and the family, nursing homes and institutionalization.

55. Myerhoff, B. "A symbol perfected in death," In B.G. Myerhoff and A. Simic (Eds.). Life's Career Aging: Cultural Variations on Growing Old, pp. 163-202. Newbury Park, CA: Sage Publications, 1978.

This chapter is set in a volume that explores crosscultural study of basic principles, processes, and cultural dynamics of aging in five different ethnocultural settings. It displays the creativity and power of ritual in binding up and expanding individual and collective continuity. Deep meaning and cohesion permeate the group.

56. Nahemow, L., McKluskey-Fawcett, K.A. & McGhee, P.E. (Eds.). Humor and Aging. New York: Academic Press, 1986.

This book presents a systematic overview of the socio-psychological role of humor in the aging process. Although it deals with humor throughout the life span, primary attention is given to humor about, for and by the elderly. The 16 contributed essays are divided into four parts which include theoretical and review material as well as empirical studies of death and dying. This volume is a valuable resource for religious professionals dealing with stereotypes, attitudes about aging and fostering intergenerational relations.

57. ** Neugarten, B.L. (Ed.). Middle Age and Aging: A Reader in Social Psychology. Chicago: The University of Chicago Press, 1968.

This classic work includes scientific studies by the pioneers in gerontology. Part III includes historical theoretical positions; Part IV, the responses to the social environment that focuses on housing; Part V includes chapters by Robert Butler on Reminiscence and David Moberg on religiosity in old age. The Appendices on research strategies remain resources for researchers.

58. Osgood, N.J. (Ed.). Life After Work: Retirement, Leisure, Recreation, and the Elderly. New York: Praeger, 1982.

This book grew out of a 1981 Conference on Life After Work held at the State University of New York at Cortland. It includes papers presented at the conference and invited chapters relevant to the topic. The volume is divided into two parts: Part I is an overview of work, past present and future, the emerging institution of retirement, and the interrelationship of work and leisure over the life cycle; Part II examines the relationship between work and retirement experiences of different subclassifications of older persons including gender differences, minorities, blue collar, white collar and professional workers. A final section deals with preretirement preparation. The chapters of this book provide religious professionals and gerontologists with historical and contemporary information about the differential experiences of retirement and leisure.

59. ** Palmore, E.B. Handbook on the Aged in the United States. Westport, CT: Greenwood Press, 1984.

The 24 contributors to the chapters deal with various groups of aged individuals in the United States. The book is divided into four parts: (1) demographic groups includes some not traditional demographic groups, such as famous aged, centenarians and veterans; (2) religious groups includes three chapters on Protestants, Catholics and Jews; (3) five major ethnic groups; and (4) special problems, seven chapters dealing with addicts and alcoholics, criminals and victims of crime, persons with disabilities, homosexuals, institutionalized and mentally ill persons and those who commit suicide.

60. ** Palmore, E.B. The Facts on Aging Quiz: Measuring Knowledge and Stereotypes. New York: Springer, 1988.

Initially developed in 1976 to stimulate interest in a course on "the social aspects of aging," the FAQ has become an international standard for measuring knowledge about aging. During the decade of the instrument's use, Palmore has revised the original quizzes and developed alternative quizzes. The volume contains an analysis of items. The frequent misconceptions on aging are included, as are the uses of the quizzes for education and research.

61. Palmore, E.B. & Maeda, D. The Honorable Elders Revisited. Durham, NC: Duke University Press, 1985.

For this revision of the 1975 edition of The Honorable Elders, intended to respond to some of the controversies and criticisms it invoked, Palmore has the assistance of Japanese gerontologist Maeda. The basic question addressed by the authors is "what is the present status and social integration of the aged in Japan?" The answers provide a test case for modernization theory, and for the first time describe basic social and attitudinal characteristics of older Japanese.

62. Parnes, H.S., Crowley, J.C., Haurin, R.J., Less, L.L., Morgan, W.R., Mott, F.L. & Nestel, G. Retirement Among American Men. Lexington, MA: Lexington Books, 1985.

Based on National Longitudinal data from the U.S. Department of Labor, the Ohio State University researchers have reported a profile of the male retiree that destroys some popular myths and provides a comprehensive view of the retired male. Some of the issues discussed are: factors affecting mortality in the years surrounding retirement; patterns of retirement; expectations and timing of retirement, leisure activities and social networks, longitudinal effects of retirement on men's psychological and physical well-being, and those who never retire. These essays will help the religious professional to understand gender differences in aging.

63. Peterson, D.A. Career Paths in the Field of Aging. Lexington, MA: D.C. Heath, 1987.

Career paths in gerontology are so diverse that newcomers to the field are often unaware of the range of opportunities that exist. Peterson's book is the first comprehensive review of the history and development of professional gerontology, the state of current practice, and the directions it is likely to take in the future. Job roles within existing service professions, as well as new opportunities for the gerontologist are described. Gerontology professionals and those considering a career in the field of aging will find this book quite helpful in assessing their skills and interests and making appropriate educational and career decisions.

64. Peterson, D.A., Bergstone, D. & Lobenstine, J.C. (Eds.). National Directory of Educational Programs in Gerontology (Fourth Edition). Washington, DC: The Association for Gerontology in Higher Education, 1987.

This 874-page Directory contains information on gerontological instruction in institutions of higher education in the U.S. and those Canadian universities which are members of AGHE. It also includes two sections based on the national survey conducted by AGHE and The University of Southern California of the extent of gerontological instruction. Section I is a quick reference guide to gerontological instruction at 3,032 institutions, the number of credit courses in gerontology/geriatrics, the number of faculty teaching gerontology, etc. Section II includes 750 full program descriptions of 376 campuses which offer four or more courses. Other information for those interested in beginning or expanding programs includes: the address of the contact person, description of the program, credentials awarded, what degree the program is attached to (if any), number of credit hours and courses required, field work requirements, and number of graduates.

65. Peterson, J.A. & Payne, B. Love in the Later Years. New York: Association Press, 1975.

This book employs research to destroy the myths about the capacity of older persons for sexual love and establish the realities within marriage and for single persons. Three chapters focus on first time marriages and remarriage. The chapter on "sexual achievement for the single person in the later years" provides information and guidance for the increasing number of single older persons.

66. Peterson, W.A. & Quadagno, J. Social Bonds in Later Life: Aging and Interdependence. Beverly Hills, CA: Sage Publications, 1985.

This volume is a collection of 21 essays that focus upon the ties that hold people together and interpret interdependent relationships. Interdependence is discussed in intimate relationships (Part I); in social support systems (Part II); and in health and social services (Part III). For the religious professional, Chapter 14 reports research on an ecumenical older adult voluntary organization's development of interdependence for individuals and an organization.

67. Regnier, V. & Pynoos, J. (Eds.). Housing the Aged: Design Directives and Policy Considerations. New York: Elsevier, 1987.

This edited book summarizes most of the important research on housing the aged and provides explicit links between research findings and their applied and policy significance. The book is organized into three sections: planned housing that serves the active elderly; supportive housing that serves moderately impaired older persons; and housing environments for frail or handicapped older persons. The chapters have identical formats that allow the reader to make comparisons between chapters. The authors discuss design issues such as residence satisfaction, promoting social interaction, facilitative management, sensory and other physiological needs of residents.

The housing issues discussed provide practical insight for religious leaders responsible for planning public and private buildings for the use of older persons as well as denominational housing for the elderly.

68. Rose, A.M. & Peterson, W.A. (Eds.). Older People and Their Social World. Philadelphia, PA: F.A. Davis, 1965.

This classic is one of the early edited works which serves as an historical base and a current stimulus. It includes Rose's chapter on "The Subculture of the Aging," Miller's "The Social Dilemma of the Aging Leisure Participant" and two chapters by Moberg on church participation and adjustment and the "Integration of Older Members in the Church Congregation." The student of religion and aging will find contemporary insights from these early publications.

69. Ruben, D.H. Drug Abuse and the Elderly: An Annotated Bibliography. Metuchen, NJ: The Scarecrow Press, 1984.

This volume is designed for those persons "familiar with elderly populations for whom substance abuse problems are potential realities." The publications annotated vary from local to national circulation, but most are periodicals and books on the subject of elderly drug abuse and addiction. The 787 entries are divided into seven topical areas: Alcohol use and abuse; illegal and legal drugs—use and abuse; epidemiology; mental health and geriatrics; drugs and alcohol; education and prevention; and, institutionalization and drug abuse. The brief introduction provides the reader with an overview of the problems addressed in the publications reported.

70. ** Schulz, J.H. The Economics of Aging (Fourth Edition). Dover, MA: Auburn House, 1988.

Written for the noneconomist as well as the economist, this volume examines the growing debate about the potential economic burden of an aging population, and the individual and policy issues that affect older persons. It includes expanded discussions of Medicare and its new prospective payment system, the future of Social Security, and the growing role of private pension, health and disability plans. As in previous editions, there are chapters on the economic status of older persons, retirement planning, and special problems of the older worker.

71. ** Silverstone, B. & Hyman, K. You and Your Aging Parent. New York: Pantheon Books, 1982.

This is an updated edition of a classic treatment of the reality of middle-aged people coping with aging parents. It includes the growing awareness of multi-generational families who are the major support system for one or more generations of older parents and relatives. In readable yet scholarly terms, this book covers the psychological and sociological dimensions of family life involving older persons. Relationships, marriage, sex, widowhood, disabilities, and death are treated as well as community services and planning for a variety of contingencies. This book will be a helpful resource to families and professionals in the field.

72. Skinner, B.F. & Vaughan, M.E. Enjoy Old Age. New York: Warner Books, 1983.

The volume is the outgrowth of a paper called "Intellectual Self-Management in Old Age" delivered by Skinner at the 1982 annual meeting of the American Psychological Association. He determined to make this a popular publication that describes behavior and feelings in old age. Since it reflects his own experience with aging and that from gerontology by Vaughan, this work is a very practical, enjoyable guide for older persons and those who are in ministry with them.

73. ** Springer, D. & Brubaker, T.H. Family Caregivers and Dependent Elderly. Beverly Hills, CA: Sage Publications, 1984.

This book bridges the gaps among researchers, practitioners, and older people and their families about caregiving responsibilities. The authors seek to translate general findings from research and specific techniques from practice for family caregivers and their older family members. This practical book can be used as the basis for discussion groups, support groups and guidance for individuals who care for dependent older persons. The objective is to maximize the independence of the dependent older person and minimize the stressful situations experienced by caregivers. A bibliography, suggested activities and a caregivers' knowledge test is included.

74. ** Tibbitts, C. (Ed.). Handbook of Social Gerontology: Social Aspects of Aging. Chicago: University of Chicago Press, 1960.

The contributed chapters represent a comprehensive survey of the field of social gerontology prior to the passage of the Older Americans' Act in 1965. Paul B. Maves' chapter "Aging, Religion, and the Church" addresses the questions about religion and aging that have been ignored for 20 years. The answers have relevance and implications for the renewed interest in the graying of congregations.

75. ** Torrey, B.B., Kinsella, K., & Taueber, C.M. An Aging World (International Population Reports Series pp. 95, No. 78). Washington, DC: U.S. Bureau of the Census, 1987.

This report summarizes detailed demographic and socio-economic statistics that have been collected on older populations in 31 countries. The data constitute the International Data Base on Aging (DBA) and are updated by the Center for International Research, U.S. Bureau of the Census. This is the authoritative resource for religious professionals concerned about national and world populations. It includes demographic trends, life expectancy, mortality and health, gender differences, urban and rural dimensions, marital and living arrangements, educational attainment and literacy, social support of the elderly, labor force trends and the economics of aging.

76. ** Waltz, Y.H. & Blum, N.S. Sexual Health in Later Life. Lexington, MA: D.C. Heath, 1987.

This volume uncovers the neglected facts that create negative myths and stereotypes about the consequences of aging for sexual functioning. Topics covered include: the value of sex after sixty; male-female differences in the effects of aging on sexuality; the effects of chronic illnesses, medical treatment, attitudes and mental states on sexual desire and capacities. It includes suggestions for encouraging sexual expression in nursing homes and community housing. It contains seven figures that minimize pain for those with painful diseases and the Adult Sexuality Knowledge and Attitude Test (ASKAT) developed by the authors.

77. * Ward, R.A. The Aging Experience: An Introduction to Social Gerontology (Second Edition). New York: Harper & Row Publishers, 1984.

One of the most frequently selected texts for undergraduate and graduate courses in the sociology of aging allows the reader to understand gerontological issues within a broad sociological framework.

78. Ward, R.A., LaGory, M. & Sherman, S.R. (Eds.). The Environment for Aging. University of Alabama Press, 1988.

This book is based on the authors' research of residential age segregation. It explores the influence of physical and social environments on the lives of older people who age in place. This includes neighborhood context, the nature and consequences of informal networks and age-related orientations. The authors report three basic themes emerging from the study: age is of limited importance and does not loom largely in the lives of the community residents; there is great diversity in the nature and implications of the environmental context; and aging must be viewed in interactional and transactional terms, i.e., older people are not simply acted upon by the environment, but experience and construct the environment as a subjective entity. The interview instrument used with 1,185 community residents aged 60 and over included in the Appendix may prove useful for the survey of parish areas.

79. ** Wilson, M. The Effective Management of Volunteer Programs. Boulder, CO: Volunteer Management Association, 1976.

The most universally used book for training practitioners who direct adult volunteer programs. The 10 chapters include: the role of the manager; motivation; organizational climate; planning and evaluation; designing jobs and recruiting to fill them; interviewing and placing volunteers; training and designing creative learning experiences; communications; the unique roles of the client, staff, volunteer and board members and their interrelationships.

Part I is Moberg's keynote address "Aging and Theological Education" presented at The National Conference on Aging, Spiritual Well-being, and Education, August 5-7, 1979 in Indianapolis, Indiana. It is a sociologist turned gerontologist's view of aging in theological education, reasons for its neglect, its need and available resources; Part II contains the guidelines for competency objectives for education for ministry in aging, interdisciplinary approaches and concerns of eight distinguished gerontologists, educators and seminary faculty members, and strategies for using the guidelines; Part III contains seven "emerging curricular models for education"; Part IV is the address of the eminent emeritus religious educator Ruel Howe on "Bringing Spirit to Aging Education in the 1980's."

THEOLOGICAL DISCIPLINES AND CLERGY PRACTICES

80. Aleshire, O. Faithcare: Ministering to All God's People Through the Ages of Life. Philadelphia: The Westminster Press, 1988.

Faithcare is an excellent resource for pastors and lay ministers who want to deepen their sensitivities to and effectiveness with persons in their congregations. What appears to be the simple task of "paying attention" to people is explored in a faith and development context that unveils a task with many complex dimensions. Aleshire offers helpful assistance in understanding and approaching faith and growth issues for children, adolescents and adults. Although this book is not focused on aging issues, the section on adulthood deals with faith development throughout life. Growth comes in later years through learning based on reaction to and reflection upon daily experience with adult tasks, roles, and events. This is learning that is dependent upon an accumulation of life experience and willingness to engage in reflection and interpretation in the "presence of God." Aleshire provides ways to understand ministry to all adults that is supportive and sensitive to need.

81. Allen, C.L. You Are Never Alone. Old Tappan, NJ: Flemming H. Revell, 1978.

A pastor emeritus of The First United Methodist Church in Houston writes about his experience of learning to live alone as his wife struggled for life over two and a half years. Allen dealt with the issues and problems "we loners" face. It is not a mournful book and he finds and shares some answers. This volume adds insights from the male perspective along with a pastor's personal and ministerial experiences and provides insight and comfort for pastors and laypersons.

82. ** Becker, A.H. Ministry with Older Persons: A Guide for Clergy and Congregations. Minneapolis: Augsburg Publishing House, 1986.

As a handbook designed to aid congregations in responding to the needs of older persons, it contains basic information on the aging process as well as practical guidelines for developing effective ministry with older persons.

It is written primarily for pastors and students preparing for the pastoral ministry. The chapters on faith concerns of the elders and ethical issues of aging provide insight for counseling with older persons and their families.

83. * Bergman, M. & Otte, E. Engaging the Aging in Ministry. St. Louis, MO: Concordia Press, 1981.

This manual for developing and organizing programs for the elderly within the local church provides a variety of options for planning and implementation. The guidelines are intended as a way of activating and involving the reservoir of skills of older people to serve the needs of the church and society. It is a practical guide for launching a senior ministry geared to resources and conditions in a local church. Attitude tests, a plan of action, goal evaluation sheet, sample information card, and a needs assessment survey are included for adaptation by others.

84. ** Bianchi, E. Aging as a Spiritual Journey. New York: Crossroads, 1984.

This study of the dilemmas posed for the human spirit by the realities of aging and death is based on interviews with retired religious educators, the author's biographical, disciplinary background and influence of Jungian psychology. The religious basis is broadly Christian with occasional excursions into Judaism and Eastern religions. The aging emphasis focus on midlife (40-60 years of age) and elderhood (above 60 years of age) as two crucial transitional periods that provide fresh opportunities for spiritual growth.

85. Bianchi, E.C. On Growing Older: A Personal Guide to Life After 35. New York: Crossroads, 1985.

This book of twenty-four meditations is intended to shape a context for experiencing our personal attitudes and feelings about aging. These are preceded by an orientation to the disciplined steps of meditation. The subjects of the reflections include loneliness, forgiving, loving, suffering, cultivation of joy, letting go, peacemaking, and being religious. These meditations could be used with a group or as an individual exploration.

86. * Boyle, S.P. The Desert Blooms: A Personal Adventure in Growing Old Creatively. Nashville, TN: Abingdon Press, 1983.

A personal account of a professional woman's experiences with aging — the shocks, the despair, the adventure of recovery and becoming a new person. The role of faith, beliefs and the church are woven throughout her account.

87. * Clements, W.M. (Ed.). Ministry with the Aging. San Francisco: Harper & Row Publishers, 1981.

The editor's stated intent is to develop the new context for ministry with the aging by paying particular attention to the process of aging without needlessly setting the aged even further apart through either idealization or trivialization. The seventeen contributed chapters form a useful and informative volume on religion and aging. The introduction sets the stage for the three sections of the book: (1) The foundation chapters provide a uniquely Christian perspective on aging. The authors discuss the religious roots and traditions from which an emergent ministry can draw and a factual basis for appreciating the presence and role of older members. (2) The chapters on challenges address the challenges facing a rapidly aging society from a Christian and Church perspective. (3) The Designs section focuses on practical applications and action approaches to ministry. The faculty, students, active clergy and lay members will find this book an excellent foundation for their responses to the emerging ministry for the aging.

88. * Clingan, D.F. Aging Persons in the Community of Faith: A Guidebook of Churches and Synagogues on Ministry to, for and with the Aging. Indianapolis, IN: Department of Aging and Community Services, Indiana Commission on the Aging & Aged, 1980.

This frequently reprinted and updated guidebook provides program models for local congregations, for teamwork between congregations and community programs. Descriptions of these programs stimulate thinking for those planning congregational and interfaith programs for the elderly. It is designed for practical use within the interfaith community.

89. Cook, T.C. (Ed.). The Religious Sector Explores its Mission in Aging. Athens, GA: National Interfaith Coalition on Aging, 1976.

This volume is the final report of NICA's Survey of Programs for the Aging Under Religious Auspices and serves as a history of NICA as an organization; Part I is the project background paper and methodology by David O. Moberg; Part II, Data, contains the research aspects of the project, the findings and implications for future research; Part III, Education, presents the general findings from the seminary survey on aging in seminary training, a survey of the literature on "Religion and Aging" and an annotated bibliography of over one hundred books and articles, and appendices which contain useful practical and historic materials.

90. * Custer, C.E. (Ed.). The Gift of Maturity. Nashville, TN: Discipleship Resources, 1986.

The seven contributed essays discuss maturing from the physical and spiritual dimensions based on an awareness that there are imbalances in striving toward maturity. The specific issues addressed by the authors from their own faith and experience are: aging as a spiritual journey; the gains and losses of aging; caring for one another; facing death; sources of strength; leaving a heritage; and being called to servanthood. Maves's Chapter 4 on facing death, is a moving factual and faith statement for religious professionals working with any age person facing death.

91. Faber, H. Striking Sails: A Pastoral-Psychological View of Growing Older in Our Society (translated from the Dutch by K.R. Mitchell). Nashville, TN: Abingdon Press, 1984.

This volume, a pastoral psychologist's study of the task and art of aging, probes what older people feel and think and their relationships with society, work, family, religion and themselves. The aging process is compared to the phases of development in youth. The final chapter focuses on pastoral care and counseling of older people and warns of the danger of writing older people off rather than viewing them as people in the middle of society who experience its problems in an acute way, who live in the present and can make contributions to society.

92. ** Fecher, V.J. Religion and Aging: An Annotated Bibliography. San Antonio, TX: Trinity University Press, 1982.

This bibliography contains over 473 annotations done by the author, including only those writings which deal with the interaction of religion and aging, or the impact of one on the other. The entries are divided into four sections: (1) the religion of the elderly; (2) organized religion in the service of the elderly; (3) spiritual ministration to the elderly; and (4) miscellaneous titles on religion and aging.

93. ** Fischer, K. Winter Grace: Spirituality for the Later Years. New York: Paulist Press, 1985.

A theologian and counselor responds to the need for a spiritual perspective to interweave with the physical, psychological, social and economic aspects of the aging process. The major theme is that "losses which accompany the aging process can lead to freedom and new life. Aging can be winter grace." The last chapter on resurrection interprets the diminishments of the last part of life through the Christian paradox of death/resurrection.

94. Fowler, J.W. Stages of Faith: The Psychology of Human Development and the Quest for Meaning. San Francisco: Harper & Row, 1981.

Based on nearly 400 interviews, this volume delineates the various ways life has meaning for persons of all ages and belief orientations. Faith is not necessarily religious nor about belief systems. Faith is defined as a human universal, interactive and social, requiring community, language, ritual, and nurture. Fowler's theory of stages is not age specific, but inclusive of all ages and developmental in the Kohlberg and Erikson tradition.

95. Gray, R.M. & Moberg, D.O. The Church and the Older Person. Grand Rapids, MI: William B. Eerdmans, 1977.

This volume is a revision of a 1962 work reporting the findings of social science research and the authors' original research on the place and function of religion in the lives of older persons. Although much research and a large number of programs dealing with religion and older people have been done which altered some of the early perspectives, the authors maintain these have not radically changed any of the basic orientations and recommendations. The revision includes updated materials and a new chapter on "The Clergy and Older People." This volume remains one of the rich resources in the practical research field of religion and aging.

96. Harris, J.G. Biblical Perspectives on Aging: God and the Elderly. Philadelphia, PA: Fortress Press, 1987.

An historical-critical study of the elderly in the Bible, which recognizes that the Bible itself had no direct interest in the question of the elderly and thus draws conclusions on rather indirect and unintentional evidence. This work has a strong ethical component that concerns social process, social practice, and social value.

Harris has walked the tightrope of biblical scholarship between the Old Testament text and the cultural, social, ethical, and theological dimensions of Israel reflected in that text. Harris explores aging issues and biblical descriptions of old age, literature of the time concerning aging, social practices which form a "common theology" of aging, and how Judaism and early Christianity both deal with the elderly.

97. Hendricks, W.L. A Theology for Aging. Nashville, TN: Broadman Press, 1986.

This "elemental theology" is written by a professor of Christian theology from a conservative, Protestant, conversionist perspective and from a confessional viewpoint. By the author's disclaimer, the book is not a scholarly, formal, academic theology, nor an analysis of the science of aging, nor a special theology for aging or aged persons that is different in substance from other Christian theologies. It is based on the experiences of normal, everyday life as analogies to express the content of theology.

98. Hendrickson, M.C. The Role of the Church in Aging for Policy and Action. New York: Haworth Press, 1986.

This volume, a special edition of Volume 2, Numbers 1/2 of the *Journal of Religion & Aging*, contains selected papers from The National Symposium on the Church and Aging sponsored by The Lutheran Council in the U.S.A. held in Zion, Illinois in 1984. Topics cover a broad range of issues from the role of the church as a generator of social and personal meaning, an enabler, advocate, and educator of older persons to how the church's facilities and resources might be better structured to serve as a primary provider of housing and formal services.

99. ** Hessel, D.T. (Ed.). Empowering Ministry in an Ageist Society. Atlanta: The Presbyterian Office on Aging, 1981.

This volume contains eight papers delivered at a Princeton Symposium with Maggie Kuhn, Carroll Estes, Richard Shaull, Heije Faber, Dieter Hessel, and Ann Hays Egan. The authors offer a critique of existing church policy and point to new direction. Two issues addressed are: (1) How much do we continue to focus on older persons' needs as such, and how much do we concentrate on mutual needs that are not age-specific?; (2) Do we want to be self-sufficient or interdependent?

100. ** Hessel, D.T. (Ed.). Maggie Kuhn on Aging. Philadelphia: The Westminster Press, 1977.

A dialogue between Maggie Kuhn, students in an advanced pastoral studies program at San Francisco Theological Seminary, and Dieter Hessel. The convener of the Gray Panthers, Maggie Kuhn served the United Presbyterian Church U.S.A. professionally for 25 years as a program executive for social education and action. In the dialogue, designed as an action guide on aging, she addresses in the dialogue the role of older persons in church and society, issues of housing, health, mandatory retirement, changing lifestyles and the church's continuing role with the aging.

101. Hulme, W.E. Vintage Years: Growing Older with Meaning and Hope. Philadelphia: Westminster Press, 1986.

A very readable book in which the author blends facts about aging with social and theological interpretations of experience. He confronts a range of societal attitudes as well as the effects of the normal aging process on the quality of the aging experience for persons today. The spiritual well-being of individuals provides meaning, purpose and a well-spring of resources for "quality aging" that can lift persons out of the cultural traps that perpetuate aging as frightening, depressing and isolating.

102. ** Kerr, H.L. How to Minister to Senior Adults in Your Church. Nashville, TN: Broadman Press, 1980.

This volume is a practical local church guide to beginning a senior adult program, improving and enlarging existing programs. Blueprintlike, the progression is orderly and easy to follow. Although it uses Baptist organizational structure, any denomination can utilize the basic strategy for program development.

103. ** Lawson, R.J. Our Congregation's Ministries With Older Adults. Nashville, TN: Discipleship Resources, 1983.

This volume is a training manual for work with older adults in the United Methodist Church. It includes steps to incorporate older adult programing into existing UMC structure, practical suggestions, models of programing separated into worship, study, service, fellowship and general areas easily adopted by local churches. Gerontological literature is interwoven with practice.

104. ** LeFevre, C. & LeFevre, P. (Eds.). Aging and the Human Spirit. Chicago: Exploration Press, 1981.

A reader in religion and gerontology organized under the headings of aging in western religious tradition, religion and aging in contemporary theology, facts and myths of aging, social science research, policy and program, and ministry to the aged.

With an emphasis on the hard questions of ultimate meaning, these theologians have looked at the reality of the aging process with images of fulfillment, personal significance, hope, and completion of life tasks. All agree that aging is a continuation of the life task of acceptance of change and growth into new meaning and purpose. Whatever informs our personal faith becomes the foundation for interpreting our experience and aging process.

105. Lewis, C.S. A Grief Observed. London: Faber & Faber Limited, 1961.

This volume is a renowned theologian's struggle with grief experienced during the long and painful illness of his wife. Lewis allows the reader to be with him, sharing his attempt to argue out his grief and the meaning of death and resurrection. This volume studied along with Allen (1978) provides a pastor's and a theologian's response to loss and death. In addition, they fill some of the gaps in the literature about the grief experience of widowers.

106. Loughhead, E.J. Eldercare: Starting a Center in Your Church. Nashville: Abingdon Press, 1987.

This is a step-by-step guide to establishing and running an effective day care center in a church. These steps include how to: get a center started; prepare the facility; recruit the staff; enroll the participants; plan a daily program; prepare a budget; support the caregiver; write to agencies for more information.

107. Lyon, K.B. Toward a Practical Theology of Aging. Philadelphia: Fortress Press, 1985.

An understanding of the relationship of human fulfillment and aging is explored as the foundation to pastoral care with older adults. The volume contains a brief discussion of the thoughts on aging of John Chrysostom, John Calvin, Richard Baxter, etc., in order to illustrate three claims: (1) old age is a blessing of God; (2) old age is a period of growth; (3) old age is to be marked by a particular religious ethical witness. The author concludes that "pastoral care with the aging involves enabling older adults to understand God's presence with them as one who blesses and one who redeems." And it "involves the building of a value-consensus within the community which affirms in word and deed God's presence with us throughout our lives."

108. Maitland, J. Aging: A Time for New Learning. Atlanta: John Knox Press, 1987.

Writing out of the conviction that God is ever present in our lives, Maitland explores the power of religious images and of images drawn from many years of each person's life experience to provide meaning and purpose in the later years. Discovery of this rich resource is a primary task of growth and learning that is not possible without accumulated years of life experience. This task builds a foundation of strength and resilience with which to face any possibilities that occur during aging. He offers practical approaches to many facets of aging as well as ways of learning to unleash the human potential present in every year of one's life.

109. ** Marshall, V.W. Last Chapters: A Sociology of Aging and Dying. Monterey, CA: Brooks/Cole, 1980.

This sociological analysis of the relationship between aging and dying includes the impact of individual and organized religion on the ways people deal with death and dying. The review of the literature is the basis of Marshall's development of a theoretical argument and an assessment of concepts from human development and gerontology including developmental theory, activity and disengagement theory, role theory and symbolic interaction. Each of the seven chapters is interpretative of the death and dying experiences in individual, social and period context.

110. ** Maves, P.B. A Place to Live in Your Later Years. Minneapolis: Augsburg Publishing House, 1983.

This volume is designed for those who have retired and will retire in the next decade and "to provide some perspective for grown children and other relatives who are concerned about how their loved ones will cope with aging, and to be usable by church, legal, fiscal and health care professionals who are called upon to solve the problems of how and where to live in later life." The focus is on the decision making process about changes in living arrangements in the context of religious faith.

111. ** Maves, P.B. Faith for the Older Years: Making the Most of Life's Second Half. Minneapolis, MN: Augsburg, 1986.

A faith-filled guide to decision making and transitions in maturity by an author who has been a researcher, practitioner and minister in the field of aging for almost 50 years.

A scholarly approach to aging is blended with a sound theological base to provide a readable expression of a faith journey into the later years. Here is a positive view of aging as a time for fulfillment and satisfaction for the individual. Stereotypes of aging are countered with the possibilities of creativity and productivity that grow out of assuming stewardship of our time, talents, bodies, social and cultural settings.

112. ** Maves, P.B. Older Volunteers in Church and Community. Valley Forge, PA: Judson Press, 1987.

A practical manual for starting a volunteer program for and with older persons, this book is soundly based in an understanding of ministry, gerontology and experience in working with volunteers. Older person ministries tap resources for the church and the community while offering older persons opportunities for personal growth and meaningful service.

113. Maves, P.B. & Cedarleaf, J.L. Older People and the Church. New York: Abingdon-Cokesbury Press, 1949.

This classic book was "the first comprehensive attempt to study the relationship of Protestant churches to people over 60 years of age." It summarizes the gerontological findings of the 1940s and the implications for pastors and church leaders. Two of the authors' research projects provide the bases for the major sections on pastoral care of and group work with older people. Although there are some period effects, the sections on pastoral care and on group work are still relevant. This volume addresses questions and issues about churches and aging that are resurfacing in the 1980s.

114. ** Meyer, C. Surviving Death: A Practical Guide to Caring for the Dying and Bereaved. Mystic, CT: Twenty-Third Publications, 1988.

This volume is based on the author's eighteen years of experience with dying persons and their families as an Episcopal priest and the Director of Pastoral Care at St. David's Hospital in Austin, Texas. The focus is on practical and emotional difficulties experienced by those involved with dying persons.

The first section deals with the dying process and offers specific suggestions for what to do and not do with the patient and family; how to make decisions about ethical issues and the technological environment of dying. The remainder of the book focuses on the caregiver and survivor. It includes a major section on "The Church and Death" and two chapters on sex after the death of a partner that address parts of the bereavement process which are omitted from most books on death and dying.

115. ** Myerhoff, B. Rites and Signs of Ripening: The Intertwining of Ritual, Time, and Growing Older. In D.I. Kertzer & J. Keith (Eds.). Age and Anthropological Theory. Ithaca, NY: Cornell Press, 1984.

An exploration of clarifying and healing public rituals and rites to help make sense of the losses which happen between retirement and funerals.

Ritual suspends time and has the power to provide important cultural roles for older persons in preserving and enhancing history, values, traditions, and social continuities.

116. Natale, S.M. Loneliness and Spiritual Growth. Birmingham, AL: Religious Education Press, 1986.

Based on empirical research, this book explores the expressions of loneliness throughout the life cycle and how loneliness can lead directly to deeper personal and spiritual growth. It includes specific intervention techniques to help persons use their own loneliness to improve the quality and power of their spiritual lives. This book provides a resource for pastors, counselors and gerontologists involved in research or practice related to loneliness.

117. ** Nouwen, H.J. & Gaffney, W.J. Aging: The Fulfillment of Life. Garden City, NY: Image Books, 1974.

A contemplative reflection on aging, enhanced by 85 photographs. The book's focus, on the interdependence of all ages, grows out of theological awareness of the wholeness of life and God's solid relationship to his creation. Healing between the generations is possible as each of us discovers our particular place in the aging process. Constraining societal stereotypes can be destroyed and new life brought into being when our own aging is faced and enlightened by the hope, humor and wisdom of those who are older.

118. * Older Adult Ministry: A Resource for Program Development. Atlanta, GA: Presbyterian Publishing House, 1987.

A loose-leaf guide for program development designed to help develop ministries by and with older adults. The first three chapters look at biblical, theological, gerontological and ecclesiastical foundations for older adult ministries. The remaining ten chapters are devoted to specific strategies for program planning and implementation.

119. ** Oliver, D.B. (Ed.). New Directions in Religion and Aging. New York: Haworth Press, 1987.

This volume, first published as two special issues of Volume 3 of the *Journal of Religion & Aging*, is a collection of articles speculating on the directions of religion and aging in the next fifty years. Part I begins by setting aside some popular stereotypes, discussions of the impact of aging on theology and pastoral care, ethics and thanatology. The final chapter addresses research needs. In Part II, specific issues are examined in the light of changing times. These include: the graying of America and the church; poverty; sexuality; suicide; intergenerational living; and community programs. Those planning ministries and worship programs for older persons will find some new directions from this volume.

120. Payne, B. & Brewer, E.D.C. A Study of the Homes Program of the Presbyterian Church (U.S.A.). Atlanta, GA: Gerontology Center, Georgia State University, 1987.

This is a study of the Homes Program of the Board of Pensions of The United Presbyterian Church, U.S.A. which was established over 100 years ago.

Although directed at the policy for the Presbyterian Church (U.S.A.), the findings about the pre and post plans and attitudes about retirement of ministers and missionaries has implications for all denominations. The research instruments are included and may be used by any researcher interested in the clergy retired.

121. ** Powers, E.A. (Ed.). Aging Society: A Challenge to Theological Education. Washington, DC: Interreligious Liaison Office, American Association of Retired Persons, 1988.

This is the culmination of AARP's project to provide assistance and a challenge to institutions responsible for training clergy and religious educators to introduce aging-related information into curricula. Scholars from Protestant, Catholic and Jewish traditions, in eight disciplines central to theological education prepared papers on aging from the perspective of their own expertise. The papers were critiqued and reviewed by two additional scholars. Disciplines included are homelitics, Biblical studies — New Testament, Biblical studies — Old Testament, pastoral care, religious education, practical theology, worship/liturgy, and theology.

122. ** Richards, L. & Johnson, P. Death and the Caring Community: Ministering to the Terminally Ill. Portland, OR: Multnomah Press, 1980.

The authors, a minister and a medical doctor, share what they did not learn in their professional education, how to deal with dying. They show how the medical professionals and the clergy, family members and members of local congregations can communicate God's love to the terminally ill. Part I discusses the needs of the terminally ill person; Part II uses models of terminally ill to sharpen the reader's sensitivity and insight to relate to the dying person; Part III is a fifteen session seminar developed as training for a congregation or families to equip them to care effectively.

123. Scudder, D.L. Organized Religion and the Older Person. Gainesville, FL: University of Florida Press, 1958.

This classic summary of the Eighth Annual Southern Conference on Gerontology contains eight papers on organized religion and older persons from Protestant, Catholic and Jewish perspectives and from social scientists and health professionals. These include Seward Hiltner's first statement on a "Theology of Aging." Social researchers Milton Barron and Ruth Albrecht's ideas explored in 1958 are just surfacing in the 1980s. There is an oldness and newness to this volume.

124. Stagg, F. The Bible Speaks on Aging. Nashville, TN: Broadman Press, 1981.

This volume, by a retired professor of New Testament at The Southern Baptist Seminary, Louisville, Kentucky, is a "careful working through" of the Old and New Testaments relative to the aging process. It organizes and discusses attitudes, stereotypes and themes about youth and age. The eight chapters cite all the references to youth and age under the following headings: Age in the Pentateuch; Age in the Historical Books; Age in the Wisdom Books; Age in the Prophets; Age in the Synoptic Gospels and Acts; Age in the Johannine Writings; Age in the Writings of Paul; and Age in the General Epistles.

125. Stokes, K. (Ed.). Adult Life Cycle. New York: W.H. Sadlier, 1982.

This volume is the product of the 1981 symposium on Faith Development in the Adult Life Cycle. The discussion and delineation of faith development goes beyond the popular interest in the changing patterns of adulthood, such as "mid-life crises," "empty nest," "baby-boom generation" and "senior citizens." It raises the question, "if everything else about us changes as we grow older, what might we expect to happen to our faith?" Fowler's (8) and Vogel's (13) chapters are of specific interest to gerontologists, seminary faculties and students interested in religion and the aging process.

126. Taylor, B. The Church's Ministry with Older Adults. Nashville: Abingdon Press, 1984.

A pastor of a large urban church in which more than half the active members were over sixty-five shares his discoveries about the remarkable resources of older members. The volume is the experience of a pastor who takes seriously the older members as active laity and the implications for developing congregational programing.

127. ** Thorson, J.A. & Cook, T.C. (Eds.). Spiritual Well-Being of the Elderly. Springfield, IL: Charles C. Thomas, 1980.

This volume is an attempt to elaborate on the concept of spiritual well-being by 30 contributors selected from the 1977 National Intradecade Conference on Spiritual Well-Being of the Elderly. The chapters are organized into six sections: (I) What is spiritual well-being?; (II) Spiritual well-being in relation to God; (III) Spiritual well-being in relation to self; (IV) Spiritual well-being in relation to community; (V) Spiritual well-being in relation to the environment; and (VI) Putting spiritual well-being into perspective.

128. ** Tobin, S., Ellor, J.W. & Anderson-Ray, S. Enabling the Elderly: Religious Institutions Within the Community Service System. New York: New York State University Press, 1986.

How can religious institutions collaborate with secular service providers to enable the elderly to remain active contributors to their communities and retain a sense of continuity in their lives? This volume represents the authors' ten years of exploring ways to answer this question and enhance the church and synagogue as service providers to the elderly. The volume is divided into three parts: Part 1. "The Context" includes four chapters dealing with aging in modern society, spiritual well-being and holistic programs with the elderly, and, an example of a community church seeking to expand its efforts to serve and enable older people; Part 2. "Serving Older People in a Variety of Settings" includes four chapters which identify diverse categories of elderly persons and their physical, social, emotional and spiritual needs. Opportunities to address these needs through collaborative programs are detailed; Part 3. "Religious Institutions and the Service System" includes two chapters on the model developed from the authors' research.

129. ** Tournier, P. Learn To Grow Old. New York: Harper & Row, 1971.

A book of personal counsel by a noted Swiss psychiatrist for those preparing to or already retired. The book concentrates on work and leisure, the need for a more humane society, the condition of the old, and aspects of Christian faith.

Informed by his personal faith in God, Tournier urges each to accept our responsibility for lifelong learning and growing, and the development of deep personal relationships. Interdependence between the ages is shown to be essential to growth at every stage of life.

130. ** Tournier, P. The Seasons of Life. Atlanta: John Knox Press, 1963.

This essay uses a parallel between the changing seasons of nature and man's unfolding life. As the seasons change and man moves from spring (childhood) through summer (maturity) and autumn (old age), he too undergoes change. Four factors contributing to this development are love, suffering, identification and adaptability. The final section addresses the meaning of life viewed from the last season.

131. ** Vogel, L.J. The Religious Education of Older Adults. Birmingham, AL: Religious Education Press, 1984.

This volume is more than a guide for developing programs and ministry to older adults. It focuses on the unique characteristics of the older learner, the learning process and educational programing that enables older adults to accept themselves as they are, to discover meaning in life as it has been experienced and to integrate all of life into the person they are.

132. ** Wilson, M. How to Mobilize Church Volunteers. Minneapolis: Augsburg, 1983.

The author recognizes that most major denominations are experiencing serious membership losses and aging congregations. The work of the church is being carried on by a handful of "faithful" who tend to "burn out" and resent the pew-sitters for their lack of involvement. She then proceeds to give a concise, easy-to-read guide for involving members of a congregation in the work of the church. The book covers the basic concept "Why Be Involved" and proceeds to an outline of "How to Involve Volunteers," including how to determine program needs, set realistic goals, organize a volunteer program, plan orientation and training for volunteers, recruit volunteers and design evaluations. In her last chapter Wilson challenges the church to reach beyond its walls and congregation and become a "scattered church in a hurting world." The appendices are check lists and examples of job descriptions, volunteer assignments, and training curricula to assist the reader in developing a volunteer program within the church.

133. Ziegler, J.H. (Ed.). Theological Education, Vol. XVI, No. 3, Special Issue. Vandalia, OH: The Association of Theological Schools, 1980.

This special issue is a dissemination of The National Interfaith Coalition on Aging's Project-Gist (Gerontology in Seminary Training) supported by a grant from the Administration on Aging in 1977-1979. It includes: an introduction and overview of the project, NICA's copyrighted definition of "spiritual well-being," four parts with contributed articles, an appendix containing lists of national consultants, participants, and organizations represented in Project-Gist and the abstracts of the participants' projects.